The
Critic

NEW MERMAIDS

General editor: Brian Gibbons
Professor of English Literature, University of Münster

Reconstruction of an eighteenth-century
stage by C. Walter Hodges

NEW MERMAIDS

NEW MERMAIDS

Richard Brinsley
Sheridan

The
Critic

edited by David Crane

Research Fellow in the
University of Wales at Lampeter

A & C Black • London
WW Norton • New York

First published 1989
Reprinted 1999
by A & C Black (Publishers) Limited
35 Bedford Row, London WC1R 4JH

ISBN 0-7136-3188-0

© *1989 A & C Black (Publishers) Limited*

A CIP catalogue record for this book
is available from the British Library.

Published in the United States of America by
W. W. Norton and Company Inc.
500 Fifth Avenue, New York, N.Y. 10110

ISBN 0-393-90058-4

Printed in Great Britain by
Whitstable Litho Printers Ltd,
Whitstable, Kent

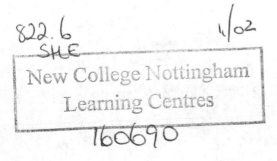

CONTENTS

ACKNOWLEDGEMENTS

I have frequently consulted the standard modern edition of Sheridan's plays by Cecil Price, although both text and commentary in the present edition have been prepared with slightly different considerations in mind. For general theatrical background, volume 6 of *The Revels History of Drama in English* and Robert Hume's *London Theatre World* have been invaluable.

I would like to thank the Librarians of the Huntington Library and the British Library for supplying photocopies without which the textual work could not have been completed. I regret that because of new managerial procedures forced upon English universities, it is not possible to thank the Research Committee of the University of Durham for any assistance received.

DAVID CRANE

INTRODUCTION

THE AUTHOR

RICHARD BRINSLEY SHERIDAN was born in Dublin in the autumn of 1751, the son of Thomas, who was himself the godson of Swift. Thomas Sheridan was a famous actor-manager (who managed nevertheless to remain a gentleman, following the example of David Garrick), and a teacher of elocution. Sheridan's mother, Frances, was a novelist and playwright of some reputation, and his grandfather, the Revd Dr Thomas Sheridan, a distinguished but financially inept schoolmaster, in whose house in County Cavan Swift finished *Gulliver's Travels*.

Thomas Sheridan's career in Dublin suffered a disastrous blow in March 1754 when a riot destroyed his theatre and ruined him (just as, in February 1809, the fire that burnt down Drury Lane ruined his son). By 1758 the family was settled in England and four years later Sheridan went to Harrow School, the son now of a struggling player and the child of a family of great talent but little social status. To be simply an actor, though a famous one, was much less than to be an actor-manager; and even though Thomas Sheridan later achieved intellectual reputation as an educator, the inventor of a distinctive elocutionary system, and the writer of a *Dictionary* (1780) and gave up the stage, his son had to make his way, both at school and after, by his own efforts.

Sheridan's career falls into two parts, theatrical and political, which can be seen clearly meshing together in *The Critic*. The period of his most intense theatrical activity and of his great creativity as a playwright began shortly after he had romantically eloped with and married the singer Elizabeth Linley. The marriage was in 1773, and two years later *The Rivals* was performed at Covent Garden (see note at I.i.227). In 1776 Sheridan followed Garrick as manager of Drury Lane, and the next year *The School for Scandal* had a highly successful run there. In another two years came *The Critic*, also at Drury Lane, so that by the time Sheridan was elected to Parliament, in the Whig interest, in September 1780, he was not only the manager of the greatest theatre in London but also the author of three of the most famous plays of the century.

In 1780, at 29 years old, he was thought a man of brilliant promise. His reputation as a speaker in the House of Commons, that other public stage, reached a high point in 1787 and 1788 during the impeachment and trial of Warren Hastings, where he made supremely good use against Hastings of oratorical talents which had been well developed by his father's elocutionary training. The rest of Sheridan's life, however, is a history of slow and eventually disastrous decline in fortune. His first wife died in 1792, and though in 1795 he married Hester Jane Ogle, the daughter of the Dean of Winchester, in spite of the fact that she was more than twenty years younger than he, his profligate habits increasingly had marked physical effects. The deterioration became steadily more evident, and the sad end of the story came with the fire at Drury Lane in 1809 and the loss of his Parliamentary seat in 1812. No longer, after the loss of his seat, immune from arrest for debt, Sheridan died with the bailiff at the door, in the most poverty-stricken circumstances, in the company of his desperately ill wife, on 7 July 1816. He was buried six days later in Westminster Abbey, not close to his lifelong friend Charles Fox (see note at I.ii.320–1), as would have befitted the politician he chiefly wished to be, but in Poets' Corner, close by Richard Cumberland, who had appeared in his play nearly forty years before as Sir Fretful Plagiary (see p. xi).

THE CONTEXT OF THE PLAY

The Critic was a play born of both a political and a theatrical consciousness. The political situation in 1779 was critical. The previous year France had recognised the independence of the United States and declared war on Britain; in June 1779 Spain followed suit, and in August the French and Spanish fleets were reported as being in the Channel (see note at I.i.5). Invasion seemed imminent, the military preparedness of the country was greatly criticised (see note at I.i.1), and an Armada spirit (much like a Dunkirk spirit) was abroad. By the autumn, however, the invasion scare had subsided, and the patriotic fervour of the earlier part of the year could be seen as excessive, though not, of course, as fundamentally unhealthy.

The theatres reacted to the political situation. In June, for instance, Sadler's Wells put on a very successful patriotic piece on the Armada theme, *The Prophecy; or, Queen Elizabeth at Tilbury* (see note at I.ii.199); but by 20 October Covent Garden (see note at I.i.227) was able to satirise the panic of the summer with a farce called *Plymouth in an Uproar*, and ten days later Drury Lane reacted to the challenge from the rival theatre with *The Critic*, hastily adapted, so it seems, for the purpose (see p. xiv and note at I.i.36). Sheridan's play matched the mood of the moment precisely. The piece we see in rehearsal in Acts II and III is Puff's tragedy, *The Spanish Armada*, a comically misconceived conglomeration of romantic love and patriotic excess; but the part of Puff was created by Sheridan's friend Thomas King, who had put together the Sadler's Wells production the previous summer (see notes at I.ii.194 and 199). Everyone was relieved that patriotic bombast could now be laughed at, and the genuine patriotic feeling with which *The Critic* ends had clearly given rise to the farcical merriment at Puff's play rather than in any way being undercut by it.

Sheridan was not only concerned, however, to react to and play upon his audience's concern with the political situation. *The Critic* is not only the theatre looking out at the great world beyond, but the theatre looking at itself, at its own world, and rightly assuming that the audience would be as intimately involved with this as they were with the threat from France and Spain. It seems likely, indeed, that as first conceived the play was simply a satire upon certain tendencies in the theatrical tradition of the later eighteenth century. There are two playwrights in the piece, apart from Sheridan himself, and the one treated with greater hostility, Sir Fretful Plagiary, was instantly recognised as a caricature of the sentimental dramatist Richard Cumberland (see notes at I.i.174, I.i.251 and I.ii.194). Cumberland's tragedy *The Battle of Hastings*, which was actually rather a success at Drury Lane in 1778 (see note at I.ii.191–3), was clearly one of the targets of *The Spanish Armada*. It is significant, however, that Sir Fretful, who is rather harshly treated in Act I, is not actually made the author of the play rehearsed in *The Critic*; after his treatment at the hands of Dangle and Sneer, he could not have survived as Puff does to conduct the seriously patriotic pageant which concludes the evening's entertainment (see notes at II.ii.471–6, III.i.287, III.i.288 sd (stage direction) and III.i.289–91).

The actor who created the part of Sir Fretful, William Parsons (1736–95), is said to have mimicked Cumberland's appearance and manner unmercifully, just as John Lacy, who first played Bayes in Buckingham's *The Rehearsal* (see note at Prologue 6), mimicked Dryden's oddities. The satire against Cumberland and his ranting theatrical writing drew, in fact, upon a tradition deriving from *The Rehearsal*, which also chiefly satirised heroic rant, a tradition so powerfully alive still in Sheridan's day that it gave a hostile energy to the attack upon Cumberland which was no doubt rather in excess of the animosity Sheridan really felt. That Puff, unlike Sir Fretful and Bayes, triumphantly survives the attack upon him and, as it were, turns the tables on the sneerers, makes Sheridan's play rather more complex than Buckingham's.

There were other theatrical targets for Sheridan, too, which had not offered themselves to Buckingham: in particular the whole genre of sentimental comedy which had replaced the licentious laughing wit of Restoration comedy in a chaster age. Sneer's friend has written a comedy 'on a very new plan' (I.i.157–72), whose object is moral reformation and whose instrument is rather tears than laughter. The degree, of course, to which tears had replaced laughter in comedies actually performed on the eighteenth-century stage can be and has been exaggerated, and it is Sheridan's intention or effect in this satire to enlarge the target area, to exaggerate the degree to which sentiment (and rant) filled the stage. It is true that Restoration bawdry was impossible in the eighteenth century and that when Restoration comedies were played they were cleaned up (see note at I.i.149), but they *were* played, and there were contemporary playwrights, too, who wrote laughing plays, as well as those, like Hugh Kelly (see note at I.i.138–9), who had more ploddingly serious concerns and who were more interested in the unlikely extremes of virtue than of vice.

What should be emphasised is that *The Critic* was written for an audience which thought the theatre important, almost as important as politics, and which would welcome the inward-turning assumption that very bad plays were as serious a threat as France, at least for so long as they watched the play; for an audience, too, which would be used to the feeling, as we all are, that politics is as *unimportant* as the theatre when set against our real private concerns. Sheridan's attack upon other parts of the theatrical world has about it an energetic mixture of seriousness and levity, hostility and joyousness; and it has an *intentness* of focus upon that world which lasts for the length of the play, perhaps because it is not intended much to outlast the play. The *Rehearsal* tradition, which gave actors in the part of Bayes the opportunity to caricature the tricks of style of fellow actors (an opportunity Garrick in particular exploited) made Buckingham's play in actual production very topical and very much of an in joke whenever it was done; and *The Critic* inherited the tradition. Carlo Delpini burlesqued himself (see note at I.ii.4–5) as Signor Pasticcio, and rather underscored than belittled his importance as a musical performer, one of the great number of Italian singers who worked in the London opera world. Similarly John Bannister as Whiskerandos (see note at I.i.319–20) is said to have alluded to William Smith's performance as Richard III, and Jane Pope (?1744–1818) as Tilburina to have been recognised as Mrs Crawford. Various newspaper reviews of the first performances of Sheridan's play make it clear that the audience picked up the references instantly. They were all in the same club, every one of them a 'dangler' (see note at I.i.1 sd), and the whole play itself was in fact a puff, whether a puff direct (see

I.ii.180–202) or a kind of puff collusive (see I.ii.246–63); just as the whole play was a patriotic piece.

The Rehearsal was clearly Sheridan's major inspiration in *The Critic*, and the audience's familiarity with Buckingham's play his chief recourse in procuring his dramatic effects. Other plays, too, similarly the offspring of Buckingham's rehearsal play, would have been in Sheridan's mind: Fielding's *Tom Thumb the Great* (1730), Garrick's *A Peep behind the Curtain* (1767), and *New Brooms!* (1776) by George Colman the Elder, among others. Behind all these, however, stood Shakespeare, like a theatrical version of the king behind his ministers, and several of Shakespeare's plays are echoed in *The Critic*, especially *Hamlet*. Shakespeare in the eighteenth century was the great justifier of the importance of the stage, and it was his plays that were most frequently performed. Cumberland, like Puff (see III.i.81–8), paid tribute by often rather grotesquely drawing upon Shakespeare, and Sheridan satirises the habit; but the matter was more complex than that. *Hamlet* itself is at times near the edge of theatrical absurdity, and the eighteenth-century audience which liked its Shakespeare entertainingly produced and with a good short piece to follow it, the afterpiece (see notes at I.i.321 and I.i.82–5), like something sweet after the main course, would have been as pleased with the degree to which Shakespeare did not transcend their rather gaudy and unsubtle taste as they were willing to enlist his authority in laughing at contemporary playwrights who were closer to the edge of absurdity. It seems probable that on the first night of *The Critic*, when *Hamlet* was the mainpiece, Ophelia was mad in white satin just like Tilburina (see III.i.234–41 and note at III.i.248–56).

The Critic was written as an afterpiece, a pendant to the main theatrical fare of the evening (even though it was in fact rather long for this purpose: see note at I.i.319–20); and it was as clearly peripheral to the political consciousness of the moment, which it lightly took up, as it was to the fortunes of the Prince of Denmark. Sheridan's very lightness of touch, however, that lack of an assertive sense of the play's own usefulness and importance (so unlike Sir Fretful's tragedy or the comedy by Sneer's friend) attracts because it does not enforce our attention, so that this little play lives as more self-consciously weighty plays of the time do not, and has outlived by far the politics and personalities of 1779. It has joined the small group of theatrical survivors, of which the greatest example is *Hamlet*, which demonstrate that the theatre at its best is indeed more important than the war with France. Sheridan was wrong to have wished in later life to be remembered as a politician rather than a poet.

THE PLAY

The Critic falls clearly into two parts. Act I, which Sheridan, according to Michael Kelly (see note at I.i.251), thought the best thing he had ever written, is a short satirical piece aimed at a whole range of different political, social and literary targets. This may well have been the full extent of Sheridan's original intention in writing the play (see *The Works of Sheridan*, ed. Cecil Price, vol. 2, p. 467); and it seems likely that it was Covent Garden's farce *Plymouth in an Uproar* (see p. x) that encouraged him to extend the play by another two acts (thus making it rather long for an afterpiece: see p. xiii), which present us with the rehearsal of Puff's tragedy, *The Spanish Armada*, Drury Lane's answer to the challenge from Covent Garden.

Act I may well have been written slowly and carefully, but Acts II and III were probably much more rapidly composed. Indeed Michael Kelly's story is often told of Sheridan being locked in the Green Room (see note at I.ii.323) two days before the first performance 'with pens, ink, and paper, a good fire, an armed chair at the table, and two bottles of claret, with a dish of anchovy sandwiches', until he had finished the play, the actors were so desperate (see James Morwood, *The Life and Works of Sheridan*, pp. 104–5). The fact also that the Examiner received a copy of the play only the day before its first performance (see note at III.i.103) is evidence of hasty, last-minute composition. The play holds together, however, and Sheridan has managed very skilfully to blend together his earlier and later inspiration into a single unified whole.

Act I opens with Mr and Mrs Dangle at breakfast, reading newspapers. The domestic world, so familiar on the stage to eighteenth-century audiences, especially with a bickering husband and wife, reaches out by means of the newspapers they are reading to the political and theatrical worlds beyond. The contrast here with Buckingham's *The Rehearsal* is marked. Buckingham's play has almost nothing in the way of a setting for the characters who watch Bayes' play. It is, to a much greater extent than *The Critic*, a disembodied literary piece. Sheridan's play is literary and political satire, but it is also a play *about* the characters who appear in it, or at least some of them, and it presents us with these characters in their human context. Of Johnson and Smith (the critical spectators of Bayes' play) we know little more than the names; Dangle, by contrast, is presented in his domestic setting, with a nagging wife and a houseful of aspirant players and Italian musicians, before he becomes instrumental as a spectator. The playwright Puff, too, whose tragedy it is we see rehearsed later on, creates for himself in Act I an elaborate social context, much more elaborate than Bayes' vestigial amours (*The Rehearsal* I.i.178–225). Of the three major characters, Dangle, Puff and Sneer, it is only Sneer who lacks context, who develops little beyond his name. Sneer, in fact, is perhaps in reality the critic in this play rather than Dangle: a man for whom the simple fact of having an opinion is sufficient justification for his existence. He springs from no human context, only a literary one, and he produces nothing himself but views. He is a parasite, and as his name declares, he derives his standing and authority from contempt for others, whereas Dangle the enthusiast (see note at I.i.1 sd) and Puff the showman draw upon a more abundant energy.

Sir Fretful Plagiary, the playwright whose tragedy we do not see rehearsed, is by comparison with the three major characters a very limited caricature. His freedom of movement within the play is severely circumscribed; he is, from the moment of his entrance at I.i.202, endowed only with the capacity to point his own moral; his function is to be easy prey for Dangle and Sneer, who themselves are allowed much more substantial stage freedom. The Italian singers of I.ii have a similarly limited role, but the limitation of their freedom is not, as it is with Sir Fretful, on account of their intrinsic absurdity, but, much more benignly (see p. xii), on account of their foreignness. Sheridan's audience may well have felt inclined to laugh at Italians because they were Italian, but this clearly is nothing like so damaging as laughing at a man because he is a fool. The humour directed at Sir Fretful Plagiary is altogether more destructive.

Sir Fretful does, however, share with Puff, Dangle and Sneer that fundamental independence of being self-invented. Indeed almost all the characters in *The Critic* are either self-invented or invented by Puff. Dangle has set *himself* up as a critic, as Mrs Dangle observes (I.i.36); Sneer, with rather greater verbal dexterity and intelligence than Dangle can command, is the virtually allegorical product of his own superciliously critical views; Sir Fretful's notion of himself as a playwright, though never allowed for an instant to prevail against the contrary opinions of Dangle, Sneer and the audience, nevertheless survives as a distinct entity. Puff, most gloriously of all, launches himself into a variety of newspaper metamorphoses (I.ii.110–61), as well as being the creator of a whole gallery of characters in Acts II and III and the showman director of the final pageant (see note on the beginning of the Prologue and at III.i.288 sd).

The heady thing about the theatre, as about politics, is that a lot can be done with words, music, costumes and scenery (whether the scene is laid at Drury Lane, Tilbury Fort or the House of Commons) to set oneself up in the eyes of the world: and Sheridan's play is really about this fundamental impulse. The force that steadily persuades *The Critic* along the path from satire towards celebration is the more and more powerfully evident sense that what animates critical spectators, playwright and the characters in Puff's tragedy alike is a single common impulse. Buckingham's play remains to the end a satire because Johnson and Smith live by an energy that has nothing in common with Bayes' enthusiasm: they are creatures from another world. All Sheridan's characters, by contrast, whether it be the wordy Sneer or the silent Burleigh (III.i.109–13), whether created directly by Sheridan or indirectly by his surrogate Puff, share the same human energy.

Puff's tragedy in Acts II and III, with the help of Loutherbourg's splendid scenes (see note at I.ii.197), comes to dominate the stage in a way that Bayes' play does not, even though it remains ridiculous. When *The Critic* was first advertised, it was offered to the public 'With New Scenes, Dresses and Decorations', most of them of course demanded by Puff's play. The scenes of Tilbury Fort and the final sea-battle (Puff's 'magnificence!' – III.i.269), attracted particular admiration: 'The scene of the battle with the Armada [was] executed in the most masterly manner. The motion of the sea, the engaging of the ships, and the destruction occasioned by the fire-ships were happily contrived and accurately represented' (*London Chronicle*, 1 November 1779). It is interesting, too, that in his minor alterations for the 1781 text, Sheridan quite often mends the metre of *The Spanish Armada* so that it *genuinely* sounds better (see note at II.ii.53). Little by little, the audience begins to forget that this absurd tragedy is to be judged contemptible, just as they forgot early on that *Hamlet* was a very unlikely tale (see p. xiii). Even the satire about politicians comes to make sense to some degree: Lord Burleigh does not speak (see note at III.i.103), but then what politician ever did speak to the people in a crisis at the moment when the real decisions were being made? Puff is right, even without the example of Lord North to help him: it is not likely 'that a Minister in his situation, with the whole affairs of the nation on his head, should have time to talk' (III.i.110–13).

And who does not know that we say absurd things when we are in love, whether in love with another human being or with our country? Puff's hold upon the audience is in reality doubly secure, since Drury Lane is full of lovers and patriots. The audience laughs, but it laughs without the edge of invective, because the target is close to home. As the play ends, it laughs at Thames between his banks (III.i.286–7), that initially ludicrous bit of Puff's final pageant which is dismissed before the pageant proper begins, but by the time we reach 'the procession of all the English rivers', the mood is unambiguously and fervently patriotic: and that mood unites everyone in the theatre, audience and players alike, in a common enthusiasm. Sheridan knew, by an instinct very like Shakespeare's, that the space between stage and audience, between theatrical life and ordinary daily life, was not great; and that if the one was a fragile illusion, then so probably was the other, with its similarly 'cloud-capp'd towers' and 'gorgeous palaces' (*The Tempest* IV.i.152); and that both needed gentle handling if they were to be real.

As a play about the theatre *The Critic* replaced *The Rehearsal*, not only because it was easier to keep it topical with constantly new touches than to dress anew a piece already a hundred years old, but because it accepted the theatre even at its most absurd as a fully human phenomenon, part of the blood-stream of late eighteenth-century London. Until quite well into the nineteenth century the play was kept topical, was kept politically and socially up to date (as, with greater difficulty, *The Rehearsal* had been), so that the acted text was never identical with Sheridan's fixed, approved printed text (see p. xxv, note at I.i.319–20 and *The Works of Sheridan*, ed. Cecil Price, vol. 1, pp. 24–8), even though the author himself almost certainly ceased to make alterations after the 1781 edition appeared.

Sheridan really lost interest in the theatre, but *The Critic*, though less popular than his two other great comedies, has steadily held the stage. As time has gone on, of course, it has become more and more a period piece, much more distinctively an 'eighteenth-century play' than ever it was when it was contemporary, and interesting in that respect to the degree that the eighteenth-century world remains interesting to us. At the heart of the play, however, there are the things that do not date: the susceptibilities of authors, the self-regarding vanities of politicians and the supercilious calm of critics.

THE STAGING OF THE PLAY

The theatre in which *The Critic* was first performed was in all essential respects Wren's building of 1674, remodelled somewhat and redecorated, but still the small and intimate place, with a capacity of about two thousand, whose passing was so much lamented when a new and larger Drury Lane replaced it in 1794 (capacity 3611) and again after the fire, in 1812 (capacity about 3000). It was said that the larger theatres too much encouraged spectacle and declamation, and coarsened the relationship between actor and audience. Richard Cumberland, in his *Memoirs* of 1806, describes how 'on the stage of old Drury in the days of Garrick the moving brow and penetrating eye of that matchless actor came home to the spectator. As the passions shifted, and were by turns reflected from the mirror of his expressive countenance, nothing was lost; upon the scale of modern Drury many of the finest touches of his art would of necessity fall short.'

The usual arrangement of an eighteenth-century stage (seen in the illustration of Drury Lane in 1777, opposite) physically separated the element of spectacle, pageant, illusion from the actor's own realistic relationship with the audience, and can be seen to fit naturally with the smaller, more intimate auditorium. The total depth of the stage was divided into the main stage, the part behind the proscenium arch, which was largely reserved for scenery and effects (it was sometimes called simply 'the scene'), and the part projecting forward from the proscenium arch, called the forestage. The main stage contained the machinery for moving scenery and actors by invisible means: it was here, for instance, that all the *traps* and *cuts* were found, the traps being square openings in the stage floor through which an actor could appear or disappear and the cuts long narrow openings running right across the stage through which scenery could rise or sink (see note at II.ii.470). The actor, however, spent most of his time on the forestage, separated from the theatrical illusion against which and not within which he played. The audience was very close to him, seated in the pit (the floor of the house) before and below him, and in the galleries and boxes round about.

This arrangement of the stage can be understood instantly as ideal for a performance of *The Critic*, which is a play sharply distinguished into man-about-town realistic chat on the one hand and overblown theatrical illusion on the other. It seems clear that the original production of the play would have made great use of the divided stage. The play opens with a brief necessary use of the scenic area behind for realistic purposes. The Dangles do not actually enter but when the curtain rises are 'discovered' at breakfast reading newspapers; but there is no doubt that they would quickly have come forward onto the forestage, Dangle perhaps rising from the breakfast table at 'Where's the MORNING CHRONICLE?' (I.1.7–8).

The first entrance in the play would have been by the servant announcing Sneer at I.i.98, with perhaps Dangle and his wife turning back a little to their breakfast room for the moment of irritation between them as Sneer is shown up. Perhaps Sneer would already have come on through a forestage entrance into view of the audience as Dangle is hissing 'You are enough to provoke –' (I.i.104), so making Dangle's discomfiture all the more comic at

The Drury Lane Theatre in 1777 (University of Bristol Theatre
Collection)

'Ha!', as he suddenly catches sight of Sneer himself and then turns awkwardly back to his wife: 'My dear, here's Mr Sneer.' The entrance of Sneer, which gives the newcomer the advantage, would then be in marked contrast with the entrance of Sir Fretful Plagiary a little later in the same scene. Here it is the character entering who is at a disadvantage: the servant takes much longer to show him up, giving time for him to be effectively ridiculed on the stage before he appears, and Sir Fretful gives immediate warning of his actual appearance at I.i.202 (in the first performance of the play the warning was given by Sir Fretful's words spoken without: see textual and commentary notes at I.i.200–1; in later performances, where Dangle is alerted to his presence before Sir Fretful actually speaks, he must instead have made some noise).

At some point about now, the inner scene of the Dangles' breakfast room has to be closed by a drop curtain, so that it can be rearranged for the next discovery at the beginning of I.ii. The change of mode of the conversation at Sir Fretful's entrance would give an unobtrusive moment for the curtain to drop, and the lengthy conversation thereafter with the playwright would allow time for a drawing room to be furnished and equipped with Italian musicians behind. Mrs Dangle goes off by a forestage exit at I.i.401 to become part of the theatrical scene behind the closed curtain. She has plenty of time to establish herself in her drawing room before the curtain rises to discover her with the Italians.

To a certain degree, the main stage at the beginning of I.ii gives us a scene like the one with which the play began; but we should notice also the change that has occurred. In the 'real-life' breakfast room at the opening of the play, the only element of theatrical illusion, that native of the scenic main stage, was in Dangle's newspaper. As the conversation between Dangle and his wife proceeded, she began to complain (I.i.57–71) of the way in which her house was turned into a theatre by his enthusiasm for the stage; and now we are actually shown the 'real-life' drawing room turned into a stage with Italian musicians, poor Mrs Dangle trapped uncomprehendingly in the midst of them. Dangle and Sneer by contrast no doubt enter at I.ii.21 through a forestage entrance, and so are at their ease passing between real-life and theatrical worlds, as they are later in commenting upon *The Spanish Armada*. With the exchanges in the first part of I.ii and the singing that follows, we have a fragment of a play within the play, preparing the way for the full-blown theatrical illusion of Puff's tragedy that comes on later.

And so enter Puff, at I.ii.48. Mrs Dangle and the Italians are ceremoniously bundled out, and the main stage closed, perhaps by a curtain, perhaps (in view of the suggestion of a painted scene in the stage direction at the beginning of II.i) by a painted drop. During

Puff's long series of speeches in the rest of I.ii (and this is why they are so long), the main stage is of course being turned into Tilbury Fort, at last coming into its own as the centre of illusion. Puff begins talking about the art of puffing, and we notice that, just as part of the stage at Drury Lane is gradually, by degrees, moving from breakfast room to romantic illusion, so part of the language of the play, which is divided as surely as the stage is, moves from ordinarily incomprehensible Italian, via Puff's new strange talk 'in the style of his profession' (I.ii.56), to its climax in the unearthly rhetoric of *The Spanish Armada*.

Dangle and Sneer exit one way and Puff another at the end of I.ii, and there must be an interval, no doubt in case more time is needed for Tilbury Fort. After the interval the same three speakers, who have by now met again in the Green Room (I.ii.323) and walked round to the front of the theatre, enter to see the rehearsal of Puff's play; Puff's 'No, no, Sir' would be an ideal way for the actor to quieten the audience. With the words of the Under Prompter at II.i.47, the whole play enters into a different relationship with the audience. From this point on, as was not the case with the Dangles' drawing room, the audience is to be aware of the mechanics by which the theatrical illusion is produced and only near the end to be decisively drawn into it and to participate. There has, for instance, been silence about the necessity for time to erect Tilbury Fort, hastily taking shape behind Puff on the art of puffing: but a little later, at II.ii.468–70, the audience, like Puff, is told about the practicalities of clearing it away (see note at II.ii.469).

The rehearsal starts, with music and the bell ringing (see note at III.i.287 sd), and II.ii discovers Tilbury Fort. From now on Puff, Dangle and Sneer are to one side of the forestage while the action of *The Spanish Armada* takes place on the main stage, with all the entrances and exits required by Puff's play being, as was sometimes said, 'within the scene', that is, not by the entrances on the forestage. The three commentating characters, each in his own different way, establish themselves as audience together with the real audience. No doubt, as well, there would have been as much opportunity for the three to upstage the players in the tragedy as there was for the real audience in a late eighteenth-century theatre at a real play. Audiences in Garrick's and Sheridan's day were a good deal less docile than they are today, less likely to respect the integrity of the theatrical production. The forestage, of course, blurred the distinction between play and audience, and there was opportunity, for instance, for that part of the audience actually seated on the stage to converse with the players and even embrace the actresses. These things were not at all unknown, though this degree of intimacy between players and audience was prevented at least at Drury Lane when Garrick remodelled the auditorium and banished spectators from the stage in 1763.

The integrity of *The Spanish Armada* is violated often as it struggles on, fighting back hard, in its constantly breached enclave of illusion. Sneer and Dangle don't like it much, the catcalling part of the audience as it were; Puff does like it, and interrupts it every bit as much with his enthusiasm, his sense that the performance fails him and his explanations of methods and effects. So when Tilburina comes in with her confidante we not only hear the music but are told the name of the piece: they are 'inconsolable to the minuet in Ariadne' (II.ii.223–4). The players interrupt the piece to talk to Puff, the prompter calls out from behind, the scene movers come in to take away bits of the sub-plot impedimenta at III.i.75–80. Besides all this, of course, the play itself, at this already particularly vulnerable point of final rehearsals when the illusion is assembled but may still be adjusted, has been dreadfully cut about before ever the performance began.

The sub-plot is introduced at the beginning of Act III. By deliberate contrast with the smoothly managed transition between Acts I and II, with plenty of time for the unobtrusive erection of Tilbury Fort, there would have been at this point, one imagines, a great deal of ill-concealed bustle and panic. The scene of the Fort has closed at II.ii.410, releasing Puff and Co to centre stage and leaving very little time for the transformation to the senate scene at the beginning of Act III. Puff, Dangle, Sneer and the Under Prompter go off at the end of II.ii, and one can imagine the delight of the real audience as the minutes tick by before the next act can begin. Eventually Puff, puffing now no doubt quite differently, appears and placates the audience with 'Well, we are ready' and the 'senate scene' is discovered. It is of course itself, in another sense, a discovery scene (see note at III.i.6).

The sub-plot is soon done with, and the main plot introduces Puff's 'principal character', Lord Burleigh, at III.i.105. Burleigh does not speak, but he does move. He comes and sits, no doubt in the centre of the main stage, on the one chair the scene movers have left for that purpose (III.i.77). Then, significantly, instead of exiting 'within the scene' like every other character so far in *The Spanish Armada*, he comes forward, according to the stage direction, and goes out (III.i.118 sd). In other words, he becomes a forestage character as he goes out, part of the audience's world, Lord North in fact (see note at III.i.103). It is hardly surprising that the reference to Lord North was instantly understood.

After Burleigh 'some of our old acquaintance' (III.i.134) reappear, and Puff's play becomes more energetically active with the scene between the two nieces and Don Whiskerandos. The eventually violent activity of the scene, the fact that the first part of it is 'aside' (III.i.150–1) to the audience, and the fact that Sir Christopher and Sir Walter, as Burleigh did earlier, come forward to avenge their nieces (III.i.162), indicates, I think, that this scene of *The Spanish Armada* is spilling out of the main stage on to the forestage; so that Burleigh has blazed the trail for the whole of Puff's play to follow. *The Spanish Armada* gathers strength, the theatrical illusion advances upon the audience, the exits and entrances required by the play are probably now by the forestage doors, and there is a great deal more exciting activity, with for instance the killing of Don Whiskerandos. At this death Puff again intervenes, asking for it to be repeated, but this has, I suggest, by now the effect of fusing together Puff and his play, the laughter and the excitement. The dead Whiskerandos walks off, the play and the play within the play now thoroughly intermingled, and enter Tilburina 'stark mad in white satin' (III.i.239–40) to remind the audience also of Ophelia and the play they have just seen (see note at III.i.248–56), Puff reading out the stage direction from the copy of his play he has in his hand. All the distinctions, between main stage and forestage, players and characters, Shakespeare and Puff, are joyously blurred, and we are prepared for *The Spanish Armada* to take its revenge upon us. De Loutherbourg's final pageant (see p. xvi) moves smoothly into place by invisible mechanical means in full view of the audience, always something greatly admired in the theatre of the time. No closed main stage and scenes discovered now, no scene movers taking away chairs, but openly impressive theatrical skill as the patriotic scene unfolds, gradually sucking the players back into the main stage (there is no provision for any other exit), the audience at least in desire and imagination following them. Puff now not like Mrs Dangle awkwardly trapped nor like Dangle beating out of time (I.ii.38 sd), but showman, linkman between theatre and audience, and himself also audience, directing and applauding. His last words, I suggest, are to the 'ladies and gentlemen' in the audience (see note at III.i.289–91), who are now content to be treated as though they were players, and who wish now, as the curtain falls closing the main stage and all the actors in *The Critic*, that they were there too behind it.

TWO MODERN PRODUCTIONS

Rather than simply listing the relatively small number of productions of *The Critic* I can discover for the period since 1945, I would like to comment in some detail about two of them. In both cases, the modern production is in an interesting relationship with the first staging of the play.

In October 1945, at the New Theatre in London, Sheridan's play followed in a double bill a performance of *Oedipus Rex* in Yeats' version of Sophocles. Laurence Olivier, who had earlier played Oedipus, was Puff. There can be little doubt, I think, though I have no direct evidence of it, that the patriotic finale of the play was given full measure and received as warmly in 1945 as I have argued it was the first time. The threat from the enemy was past by the late summer of that year as it had been by the time of the performance in October 1779, and the threat had been deadly. Where unease was felt seems to have been in the yoking together of Sophocles and Sheridan; it was clearly more difficult in 1945 than it had been in the eighteenth century to hold together so closely tragedy and comedy. 'Would Irving have followed Hamlet with Jingle?' James Agate asked (*The Contemporary Theatre*, 1946, p. 231), perhaps unaware of what Sheridan himself had done the first night. This critical reaction was more solemn, less flexible, less Shakespearean (for Shakespeare would surely have understood Ophelia and Tilburina); but by contrast it was not difficult, if I am right, to allow proper patriotism to emerge at the end of the war from a comic context.

Forty years on, in September 1985, the National Theatre version of *The Critic* followed Tom Stoppard's *The Real Inspector Hound*, with Ian McKellen as Puff and Inspector Hound. The tensely present possibility of the serious that Sheridan would have recognised in the New Theatre production, where his play followed and derived some of its energies from a war and a great tragedy, had disappeared in this later version and setting of the play. No great tragedy, no war, and certainly no serious patriotism: Puff's final pageant, his magnificence, collapsed about him to the strains of 'Rule Britannia'. The audience in 1945, and certainly the energetically patriotic audience of 1779, would never have allowed burlesque this easy latitude. Perhaps though – a final thought – the audience for the first night of *The Rehearsal*, in December 1671, easily and utterly contemptuous of Bayes as they were encouraged to be, would have been secure enough in their newly restored comforts to allow comedy such an unsubtle triumph in this play as well. Sheridan, I have suggested, wrote a more sophisticated play for a less comfortable audience.

THE TEXT

A copy of the first printed version of *The Critic*, for T. Becket 1781, now in the British Library (BL: 1342.o.13.(2.)), provides the copy text for this edition (this particular British Library copy has an 's' failing to print at the end of a line at II.ii.321, as the textual note records; other copies of the 1781 printing may very well not show this clearly progressive damage). Sheridan himself authorised the printed version of 1781 by contributing a preface to it, addressed to Mrs Greville. The text is virtually free of difficulty. It has been collated, however, with the earliest extant manuscript of the play, which was the copy submitted for licensing to the Lord Chamberlain on Friday, 29 October 1779, the day before the first performance (see note at III.i.103). This is now Larpent MS 494 in the Huntington Library. It is clear that the play as variously acted during Sheridan's lifetime differed in many respects from the play as printed in 1781, and the recording of significant variants in the Lord Chamberlain's copy, which represents the earliest acting version, gives a good view of the kind of difference to be expected between versions of the play as it responded to the immediate needs of this or that production. Attention is often drawn to the textual notes in the commentary, because a good deal can be learnt, particularly about the evolving theatrical presence of the play, from the detailed pattern of variation between versions, even though not all the changes in the later text represent *production* improvements; some are simply variants suitable for the printed and not the performed version of the play, or changes introduced for topical reasons. The standard modern edition of Sheridan's text is by Cecil Price (Oxford, 1973), and I have consulted this, though not always coming to the same conclusions (readings accepted from Price are marked 'ed'.). The capitalisation of the 1781 text has been preserved unchanged (though not in stage directions, and not in two other instances, at I.ii.243, where capitals have been introduced), on the grounds that the capitalisation contributes importantly to the reader's sense of the flavour of the text he is reading, its accents and patterns of stress. Otherwise, spelling and punctuation have been silently modernised, except on occasion in the play within the play and in Sheridan's attempts at Italian, where either the original spelling is clearly part of the joke or the text is so erroneous as to need correction in a commentary note. At other times, where the copy text has been corrected rather than modernised, a textual note records this. In the textual notes 1781 refers to the copy-text and L to the Larpent MS.

FURTHER READING

The standard modern editions of Sheridan's plays and letters are: *The Dramatic Works of Richard Brinsley Sheridan,* ed. Cecil Price, 2 vols (Oxford, 1973) and *The Letters of Richard Brinsley Sheridan,* ed. Cecil Price, 3 vols (Oxford, 1966).

There are a number of twentieth-century biographies. The following represent a variety of different approaches: Walter Sichel, *Sheridan* (London, 1909); R. Crompton Rhodes, *Harlequin Sheridan* (Oxford, 1933); and James Morwood, *The Life and Works of Richard Brinsley Sheridan* (Edinburgh, 1985). Morwood contains an illuminating critical discussion of the plays, but other useful critical accounts should be mentioned: Mark S. Auburn, *Sheridan's Comedies* (Nebraska, 1977); John Loftis, *Sheridan and the Drama of Georgian England* (Cambridge, Mass., 1977); and *Sheridan: comedies: a casebook*, ed. P. Davison (Basingstoke, 1986). Recent work on Sheridan also includes: *Sheridan Studies,* ed. James Morwood & David Crane (Cambridge, 1995).

More general background reading should include factual theatre history, such as: Philip H. Highfill Jr et al., *A Biographical Dictionary of Actors, Actresses, Musicians, Dancers, Managers and Other Stage Personnel in London, 1660-1800* (Carbondale, 1973–93); Michael R. Booth et al., *The Revels History of Drama in English,* vol. 6 (London,1975); and *The London Theatre World, 1660-1800,* ed. Robert D. Hume (Carbondale, 1980), and also more critical accounts of trends and developments: D. F. Smith, *Plays about the Theatre in England* (London, 1936); V. C. Clinton-Baddeley, *The Burlesque Tradition in the English Theatre after 1660* (London, 1952); D. F. Smith, *The Critics in the Audience of the London Theatres from Buckingham to Sheridan* (Albuquerque, 1953); Arthur Sherbo, *English Sentimental Drama* (East Lansing, Mich., 1957); Cecil Price, *Theatre in the Age of Garrick* (Oxford, 1973); and Richard Bevis, *The Laughing Tradition* (London, 1980).

Opposite: Title page of the 1781 edition of *The Critic,* reproduced by courtesy of the British Library

THE
CRITIC
OR
A Tragedy Rehearsed

A
Dramatic Piece

in three ACTS

as it is performed at the

THEATRE ROYAL in DRURY LANE

By
Richard Brinsley Sheridan Esq.

LONDON,

Printed for T. Becket, Adelphi, Strand,

MDCCLXXXI.

TO Mrs GREVILLE

MADAM,

In requesting your permission to address the following
pages to you, which as they aim themselves to be critical,
require every protection and allowance that approving taste
or friendly prejudice can give them, I yet ventured to mention
no other motive than the gratification of private friendship   5
and esteem. Had I suggested a hope that your implied
approbation would give a sanction to their defects, your
particular reserve, and dislike to the reputation of critical
taste, as well as of poetical talent, would have made you
refuse the protection of your name to such a purpose.   10
However, I am not so ungrateful as now to attempt to combat
this disposition in you. I shall not here presume to argue that
the present state of poetry claims and expects every assistance
that taste and example can afford it: nor endeavour to prove
that a fastidious concealment of the most elegant productions   15
of judgment and fancy is an ill return for the possession of
those endowments. – Continue to deceive yourself in the idea
that you are known only to be eminently admired and
regarded for the valuable qualities that attach private
friendships, and the graceful talents that adorn conversation.   20
Enough of what you have written, has stolen into full public
notice to answer my purpose; and you will, perhaps, be the
only person, conversant in elegant literature, who shall read
this address and not perceive that by publishing your
particular approbation of the following drama, I have a more   25
interested object than to boast the true respect and regard
with which

> I have the honour to be,
>   MADAM,
>   Your very sincere,   30
>   And obedient humble servant,
>   R. B. SHERIDAN.

Dedication: To Mrs GREVILLE Frances Greville (?–1789) was the mother of
  Sheridan's mistress, Mrs Frances Anne Crewe (1748–1818), the dedicatee of
  The School for Scandal.
19 *attach* attract and secure
21–2 *public notice* Mrs Greville was well known for her ode entitled 'A Prayer for
  Indifference', said to have been inspired by the infidelities of her husband.
26 *interested object* self-interested concern

PROLOGUE

By the Honourable RICHARD FITZPATRICK.

The Sister Muses, whom these realms obey,
Who o'er the Drama hold divided sway,
Sometimes, by evil counsellors, 'tis said
Like earth-born potentates have been misled:
In those gay days of wickedness and wit,   5
When Villiers criticized what Dryden writ,
The Tragic Queen, to please a tasteless crowd,
Had learned to bellow, rant, and roar so loud,
That frightened Nature, her best friend before,
The blustering beldam's company forswore.   10
Her comic Sister, who had wit 'tis true,
With all her merits, had her failings too;
And would sometimes in mirthful moments use
A style too flippant for a well-bred Muse.
Then female modesty abashed began   15
To seek the friendly refuge of the fan,

1–4 *The . . . misled*: 1781 (*omits* L)
7 *crowd* L (crow'd 1781)

Prologue: RICHARD FITZPATRICK Richard Fitzpatrick (1748–1813) was the second son
of the 1st Earl of Upper Ossory and, with Sheridan, a friend of Charles Fox; the
circle also included Mrs Crewe and George Selwyn (1719–91). See notes at
I.ii.232, I.ii.320–1 and III.i.283. The Prologue was spoken by Thomas King,
who thus as Puff both begins and ends the play (see notes at I.ii.194 and
III.i.289–91).
1 *Sister Muses* Melpomene (the muse of tragedy) and Thalia (the muse of
comedy), daughters of Zeus and Mnemosyne, preside over the theatrical
kingdom.
6 *Villiers* George Villiers, 2nd Duke of Buckingham (1628–87), wrote a play
called *The Rehearsal* that satirised Dryden and other playwrights and whose
main character was Bayes, an author. This was first performed at Drury Lane
on 7 December 1671, a little over a hundred years before the first performance
of *The Critic* in the same place, and it remained steadily popular and very well
known to audiences; Garrick, for instance, played the part of Bayes almost fifty
times. Sheridan's play very frequently echoes Buckingham's similar burlesque
of a play rehearsal, and the success of *The Critic* finally brought to an end the
long success of the earlier play.
10 *beldam* virago

Awhile behind that slight entrenchment stood,
Till driven from thence, she left the stage for good.
In our more pious, and far chaster times,
These sure no longer are the Muse's crimes!   20
But some complain that, former faults to shun,
The reformation to extremes has run.
The frantic hero's wild delirium past,
Now insipidity succeeds bombast;
So slow Melpomene's cold numbers creep,   25
Here dullness seems her drowsy court to keep,
And we are scarce awake, whilst you are fast asleep.
Thalia, once so ill behaved and rude,
Reformed, is now become an arrant prude,
Retailing nightly to the yawning pit,   30
The purest morals, undefiled by wit!
Our Author offers in these motley scenes,
A slight remonstrance to the Drama's queens,
Nor let the goddesses be over nice;
Free spoken subjects give the best advice.   35
Although not quite a novice in his trade,
His cause tonight requires no common aid.
To this, a friendly, just, and powerful court,
I come Ambassador to beg support.
Can he undaunted, brave the critic's rage?   40
In civil broils, with brother bards engage?
Hold forth their errors to the public eye,
Nay more, e'en Newspapers themselves defy?
Say, must his single arm encounter all?
By numbers vanquished, e'en the brave may fall;   45

19 *times,* (times! 1781; Times, L)
26 *Here...court* 1781 (Her drowsy Court here Dulness seems L)
38-9 *To...support.* 1781 (*these lines transferred to follow line 45* L)

---

17 *slight entrenchment* The fragile defensive outwork against embarrassment
provided by a fan covering the face. The use of military imagery in this
prologue was particularly appropriate to the time.
25 *numbers* lines of verse
27 *And we...asleep* The long Alexandrine, surrounded as it is by shorter, brisker
lines, gives a sleepy effect.
30 *pit* The pit was traditionally thought of as the abode of the professional critics,
and as the eighteenth century went on it became increasingly too a fashionable
place from which to watch a play.
34 *nice* delicate
36 *not quite a novice* Sheridan by this time had already written *The Rivals* (1775)
and *The School for Scandal* (1777).
45 *numbers* now not in the sense of line 25

And though no leader should success distrust,
Whose troops are willing, and whose cause is just;
To bid such hosts of angry foes defiance,
His chief dependance must be, YOUR ALLIANCE.

DRAMATIS PERSONAE

Dangle	Mr DODD
Sneer	Mr PALMER
Sir Fretful Plagiary	Mr PARSONS
Signor Pasticcio Ritornello	Mr DELPINI
Interpreter	Mr BADDELEY
Under Prompter	Mr PHILLIMORE

AND

Puff	Mr KING
Mrs Dangle	Mrs HOPKINS
Italian Girls	Miss FIELD, and the Miss ABRAMS

Characters of the TRAGEDY

Lord Burleigh	Mr MOODY
Governor of Tilbury Fort	Mr WRIGHTEN
Earl of Leicester	Mr FARREN
Sir Walter Raleigh	Mr BURTON
Sir Christopher Hatton	Mr WALDRON
Master of the Horse	Mr KENNY
Beefeater	Mr WRIGHT
Justice	Mr PACKER
Son	Mr LAMASH
Constable	Mr FAWCETT
Thames	Mr GAWDRY

AND

Don Ferolo Whiskerandos	Mr BANNISTER, jun.
1st Niece	Miss COLLET
2nd Niece	Miss KIRBY
Justice's Lady	Mrs JOHNSTON
Confidante	Mrs BRADSHAW

AND

Tilburina	Miss POPE

Guards, Constables, Servants, Chorus, Rivers, Attendants, &c. &c.

THE CRITIC

Act I, Scene i

MR *and* MRS DANGLE *at breakfast, and reading newspapers*

DANGLE (*reading*)
'BRUTUS to LORD NORTH.' – 'Letter the second, on the
STATE OF THE ARMY.' – Pshaw! 'To the first L dash D of the
A dash Y.' – 'Genuine Extract of a Letter from ST
KITTS.' – 'COXHEATH INTELLIGENCE.' – 'It is now confi-
dently asserted that SIR CHARLES HARDY.' – Pshaw!   5
– Nothing but about the fleet, and the nation! – and I hate
all politics but theatrical politics. – Where's the MORNING
CHRONICLE?
MRS DANGLE
Yes, that's your gazette.
DANGLE
So, here we have it. – 'Theatrical intelligence extraordin-   10

---

4 *INTELLIGENCE*.' 1781 (*Intelligence* – Pshaw! Politics! L)

1 sd *DANGLE* A 'dangler' was a follower, an enthusiast.
   reading newspapers The importance of newspapers is clear in this play. Sheridan
   himself with others in 1779 launched an opposition periodical called *The
   Englishman*.
1 *BRUTUS* One of the pseudonyms of the Whig letter writer, probably Sir Philip
   Francis (1740–1818), who under the name of Junius attacked among others
   Lord North, George III's Prime Minister from 1779 to 1782, in a series of
   letters written to the *Public Advertiser* between 1769 and 1771. 'Brutus' had
   written to the editor of the *Public Advertiser* on 6 September 1779 criticising the
   military preparedness of the Westminster and Middlesex volunteers who had
   gathered at Coxheath near Maidstone under the Duke of Devonshire to meet
   the threat from France, which had in 1778 recognised the independence of the
   United States and declared war on Britain.
2–3 *first L dash D of the A dash Y* John Montagu, Earl of Sandwich (1718–92),
   first Lord of the Admiralty
3–4 *ST KITTS* See note at I.ii.316.
4 *COXHEATH* The camp at Coxheath became more a place for fashionable patriotic
   fervour than serious military preparation, and was one of the topical interests of
   the 1778 theatre season.
5 *SIR CHARLES HARDY* (?1716–80) Commander of the Channel Fleet, who was
   ineffectual in opposing the French and Spanish ships in August 1779.
7–8 *MORNING CHRONICLE* A Whig newspaper founded and edited (until 1789) by
   William Woodfall (1746–1803), who was also its careful and conscientious
   dramatic critic.
9 *gazette* Dangle has been disgustedly reading the *London Gazette*, a government
   newspaper giving information about public appointments and official matters.

ary.'–'We hear there is a new tragedy in rehearsal at Drury
Lane Theatre, called the SPANISH ARMADA, said to be
written by Mr PUFF, a gentleman well known in the
theatrical world; if we may allow ourselves to give credit to
the report of the performers, who, truth to say, are in   15
general but indifferent judges, this piece abounds with
the most striking and received beauties of modern composition.'–So! I am very glad my friend PUFF's tragedy is
in such forwardness.–Mrs Dangle, my dear, you will be
very glad to hear that PUFF's tragedy–   20
MRS DANGLE
Lord, Mr Dangle, why will you plague me about such
nonsense?–Now the plays are begun I shall have no
peace.–Isn't it sufficient to make yourself ridiculous by
your passion for the theatre, without continually teasing me
to join you? Why can't you ride your hobby-horse without   25
desiring to place me on a pillion behind you, Mr Dangle?
DANGLE
Nay, my dear, I was only going to read–
MRS DANGLE
No, no; you never will read anything that's worth listening
to:–you hate to hear about your country; there are letters
every day with Roman signatures, demonstrating the   30
certainty of an invasion, and proving that the nation is

17–18 *composition.*' (composition' 1781; Composition, tho' truth to say we had
    rather see Tragedy on principles diametrically opposite L)

---

12 SPANISH ARMADA Spain joined France and declared war on England in June
    1779; there was briefly great alarm, but by the time the new season began the
    Spanish threat was matter, as here, for comedy.
17 *received* approved
19 *in such forwardness* so nearly ready for performance
22 *plays are begun* The theatrical season began each year as people came back to
    town for the beginning of Michaelmas term; the social season was linked to the
    legal terms. A regular season would normally last about thirty weeks, but might
    be extended through May and into June. After 1766 there was also a licensed
    summer theatre.
25 *hobby-horse* A battle is fought in *The Rehearsal* 'between foot and great Hobby
    horses' (V.i.328); and the hero, Bayes, refers at I.i.308–9 to critics as hobby-
    horses (see note at I.i.36: all references to *The Rehearsal* are to the edition by
    D. E. L. Crane, Durham, 1976).
30 *Roman signatures* Writing letters to the editor under Roman pseudonyms was
    common, and there was a spate of them in September 1779, commenting on the
    country's inadequate defences.

utterly undone – But you never will read anything to
entertain one.

DANGLE
What has a woman to do with politics, Mrs Dangle?

MRS DANGLE
And what have you to do with the theatre, Mr Dangle?   35
Why should you affect the character of a Critic? I have no
patience with you! – haven't you made yourself the jest of
all your acquaintance by your interference in matters where
you have no business? Are not you called a theatrical
Quidnunc, and a mock Maecenas to second-hand authors?   40

DANGLE
True; my power with the Managers is pretty notorious; but
is it no credit to have applications from all quarters for my
interest? – From lords to recommend fiddlers, from ladies
to get boxes, from authors to get answers, and from actors
to get engagements.   45

MRS DANGLE
Yes, truly; you have contrived to get a share in all the
plague and trouble of theatrical property, without the
profit, or even the credit of the abuse that attends it.

DANGLE
I am sure, Mrs Dangle, YOU are no loser by it, however; YOU
have all the advantages of it: – mightn't you, last winter,   50
have had the reading of the new Pantomime a fortnight
previous to its performance? And doesn't Mr Fosbrook let
you take places for a play before it is advertised, and set
you down for a Box for every new piece through the
season? And didn't my friend, Mr Smatter, dedicate his last   55

33 *entertain* Mrs Dangle's concern seems not itself very agonised.
36 *character of a Critic* Bayes loathes critics: 'there are, now-a-days, a sort of
    persons, they call Critiques, that, I gad, have no more wit in them than so many
    Hobby-horses; but they'll laugh you, Sir, and find fault, and censure things'
    (*The Rehearsal* I.i.307–10). Sheridan's spelling of the word 'critic' without the
    final 'k' occasioned comment. The story was told in the *Morning Chronicle* of 15
    December 1779 that Sheridan meant to intimate by this short spelling on the
    play bills 'that the Piece was not *finished* when the bills were printed' (see p.
    xiv).
40 *Quidnunc* from *quid nunc?* what now? – a newsmonger, a gossip
    Maecenas the patron of Virgil and Horace, and so a name for any literary patron
    second-hand unoriginal
43 *interest* influence
52 *Mr Fosbrook* Thomas Fosbrook (?–c.1830) was numberer (the man who
    counted the audience to see that the number tallied with ticket receipts), box
    bookkeeper and housekeeper at Drury Lane for many years. It was his function
    to take reservations for seats.

Farce to you at my particular request, Mrs Dangle?

MRS DANGLE

Yes; but wasn't the Farce damned, Mr Dangle? And to be
sure it is extremely pleasant to have one's house made the
motley rendezvous of all the lackeys of literature! – The
very high change of trading authors and jobbing   60
critics! – Yes, my drawing room is an absolute register
office for candidate actors, and poets without character; –
then to be continually alarmed with Misses and Ma'ams
piping hysteric changes on JULIETS and DORINDAS, POLLYS
and OPHELIAS; and the very furniture trembling at the   65
probationary starts and unprovoked rants of would-be
RICHARDS and HAMLETS! – And what is worse than all, now
that the Manager has monopolized the Opera House,
haven't we the Signors and Signioras calling here, sliding
their smooth semibreves, and gargling glib divisions in their 70
outlandish throats – with foreign emissaries and French
spies, for aught I know, disguised like fiddlers and figure
dancers!

DANGLE

Mercy! Mrs Dangle!

MRS DANGLE

And to employ yourself so idly at such an alarming crisis as 75
this too – when, if you had the least spirit, you would have

---

68 *Manager has* 1781 (Managers have L)

57 *damned* condemned, driven off the stage
60 *high change* Like the Stock Exchange, where 'traders' and 'jobbers' conducted
their business. The Royal Exchange was repaired and beautified in 1769.
62 *without character* This could mean 'not in any way outstanding or distinctive',
but is more likely to mean 'unrecommended', like a servant girl applying to Mrs
Dangle for a position without a reference or 'character'.
64 *DORINDAS, POLLYS* Dorinda is a character in Farquhar's *The Beaux' Stratagem*
(1707), Polly Peachum in Gay's *The Beggar's Opera* (1728).
68 *Manager . . . House* Haymarket Opera House (King's Theatre) was bought by
Sheridan and Thomas Harris in February 1778; Harris soon withdrew, and
Sheridan sold his interest in November 1781. The textual note indicates that
there were two managers in 1779 and one by 1781. The episode with the Italian
singers in I.ii no doubt draws on Sheridan's own experience at the King's
Theatre with opera production.
69–70 *sliding . . . semibreves* gliding from note to note in the sing-song Italian
manner
70 *divisions* florid passages of melody

been at the head of one of the Westminster associations – or
trailing a volunteer pike in the Artillery Ground! – But
you – o' my conscience, I believe if the French were landed
tomorrow, your first enquiry would be, whether they had   80
brought a theatrical troupe with them.

DANGLE

Mrs Dangle, it does not signify – I say the stage is 'the
Mirror of Nature', and the actors are 'the Abstract, and
brief Chronicles of the Time': – and pray what can a man of
sense study better? – Besides, you will not easily persuade   85
me that there is no credit or importance in being at the head
of a band of critics, who take upon them to decide for the
whole town, whose opinion and patronage all writers
solicit, and whose recommendation no manager dares
refuse!   90

MRS DANGLE

Ridiculous! – Both managers and authors of the least merit
laugh at your pretensions. – The PUBLIC is their CRI-
TIC – without whose fair approbation they know no play can
rest on the stage, and with whose applause they welcome
such attacks as yours, and laugh at the malice of them,   95
where they can't at the wit.

DANGLE

Very well, Madam – very well.

                           Enter SERVANT

SERVANT

Mr Sneer, Sir, to wait on you.

DANGLE

O, show Mr Sneer up.   *Exit* SERVANT
Plague on't, now we must appear loving and affectionate,   100
or Sneer will hitch us into a story.

82–5 – *I say . . . persuade* 1781 (, you will never persuade L)

77–8 *Westminster . . . Ground*   The Westminster associations were volunteer
    militia formed to meet the crisis with France and Spain; and the Artillery
    Ground was a place for military exercise just north of Moorfields in London.
82–5 *the stage . . . better* These two references to *Hamlet* (III.ii and II.ii) do not, as
    the textual note makes clear, occur in the manuscript of *The Critic* submitted to
    the Lord Chamberlain the day before the first performance. The mainpiece on
    the first night of the play was *Hamlet*, however, and it seems clear that the
    references passed into Sheridan's text at the moment of performance, although
    the frequent echoes of Shakespeare's play in Puff's tragedy later in *The Critic*
    make it clear that *Hamlet* was often in Sheridan's mind as he wrote. No doubt
    Hamlet was chosen as the mainpiece on the first night for this reason. See also
    the note at III.i.81.
101 *hitch us into a story* make us the gossip of the town

MRS DANGLE
With all my heart; you can't be more ridiculous than you
are.
DANGLE
You are enough to provoke –

Enter MR SNEER

– Ha! my dear Sneer, I am vastly glad to see you. My dear,   105
here's Mr Sneer.
MRS DANGLE
Good morning to you, Sir.
DANGLE
Mrs Dangle and I have been diverting ourselves with the
papers. – Pray, Sneer, won't you go to Drury Lane theatre
the first night of Puff's tragedy?   110
SNEER
Yes; but I suppose one shan't be able to get in, for on the
first night of a new piece they always fill the house with
orders to support it. But here, Dangle, I have brought you
two pieces, one of which you must exert yourself to make
the Managers accept, I can tell you that, for 'tis written by a 115
person of consequence.
DANGLE
So! now my plagues are beginning!
SNEER
Aye, I am glad of it, for now you'll be happy. Why, my dear
Dangle, it is a pleasure to see how you enjoy your volunteer
fatigue, and your solicited solicitations.   120
DANGLE
It's a great trouble – yet, egad, it's pleasant too. – Why,
sometimes of a morning, I have a dozen people call on me
at breakfast time, whose faces I never saw before, nor ever
desire to see again.

---

121 *it's* L (its 1781)

---

102 *With all my heart* Mrs Dangle cares little for Dangle's anxiety, and seems even
    to welcome the prospect of a story told by Sneer.
112-13 *with orders to support it* The custom, freely practised at Drury Lane while
    Sheridan was manager, was to give free admission (and not only on the first
    night) to certain of the audience who would applaud the play; part of the 'Art of
    Puffing' (see I.ii.283-4). Bayes' friends, too, are 'ready in the Pit' to clap (*The
    Rehearsal* I.i.297).
120 *solicited solicitations* asking for the favourable notice he has been asked to ask
    for

SNEER

That must be very pleasant indeed!   125

DANGLE

And not a week but I receive fifty letters, and not a line in
them about any business of my own.

SNEER

An amusing correspondence!

DANGLE (*reading*)

'Bursts into tears, and exit.' What, is this a tragedy?

SNEER

No, that's a genteel comedy, not a translation – only *taken*   130
from the French; it is written in a style which they have
lately tried to run down; the true sentimental, and nothing
ridiculous in it from the beginning to the end.

MRS DANGLE

Well, if they had kept to that, I should not have been such
an enemy to the stage; there was some edification to be got   135
from those pieces, Mr Sneer!

SNEER

I am quite of your opinion, Mrs Dangle; the theatre, in
proper hands, might certainly be made the school of
morality; but now, I am sorry to say it, people seem to go
there principally for their entertainment!   140

MRS DANGLE

It would have been more to the credit of the Managers to
have kept it in the other line.

SNEER

Undoubtedly, Madam, and hereafter perhaps to have had it

---

129 *'Bursts . . . exit.'* 1781 (*omits* L)

---

129 *Bursts . . . exit* Dangle's short quotation from the new comedy, not in the
original version of the play, makes the joke more vivid for an audience. Many of
the variants between L and 1781 can be explained similarly.

130–1 *taken from the French* The operative word is 'taken'. A translation
acknowledges its original; this does not. The audience would remember Bayes'
Rule of Transversion, his method of plagiarising (*The Rehearsal* I.i.96–112).
Sheridan, like Buckingham, was much concerned with plagiarism, as witness Sir
Fretful's surname, and amusingly refers to the charges of it levelled against
himself when he makes Sir Fretful wary of submitting a play to a theatre
manager who *'writes himself'* (I.i.232).

138–9 *school of morality* Winworth, at the end of Hugh Kelly's *False Delicacy*
(1768), says 'the stage should be a school of morality'.

140 *entertainment* Mrs Dangle is better entertained (I.i.33) by wars and rumours of
wars. Oddly, she seems to think the theatre ought to be a more serious place
than the battlefield. Dangle himself is perhaps less muddled.

142 *in the other line* of the other sort

recorded, that in the midst of a luxurious and dissipated
age, they preserved *two* houses in the capital, where the 145
conversation was always moral at least, if not entertaining!

DANGLE

Now, egad, I think the worst alteration is in the nicety of
the audience. – No double entendre, no smart innuendo
admitted; even Vanbrugh and Congreve obliged to undergo
a bungling reformation! 150

SNEER

Yes, and our prudery in this respect is just on a par with the
artificial bashfulness of a courtesan, who increases the
blush upon her cheek in an exact proportion to the
diminution of her modesty.

DANGLE

Sneer can't even give the Public a good word! – But what 155
have we here? [*reading*] – This seems a very odd –

SNEER

O, that's a comedy on a very new plan; replete with wit and
mirth, yet of a most serious moral! You see it is called 'THE
REFORMED HOUSEBREAKER'; where, by the mere force of
humour, HOUSEBREAKING is put into so ridiculous a light, 160
that if the piece has its proper run, I have no doubt but that
bolts and bars will be entirely useless by the end of the
season.

DANGLE

Egad, this is new indeed!

SNEER

Yes; it is written by a particular friend of mine, who has 165
discovered that the follies and foibles of society are subjects
unworthy the notice of the Comic Muse, who should be
taught to stoop only at the greater vices and blacker crimes
of humanity – gibbeting capital offences in five acts, and
pillorying petty larcenies in two. – In short, his idea is to 170

---

145 *two houses* The 'houses' Sneer refers to are the two principal theatres in
  London, Drury Lane and Covent Garden (see note at I.i.227) where, by
  contrast with the houses people actually lived in all over London, moral
  standards would be upheld. The contrast in the late eighteenth century between
  the way people actually lived and the moral delicacy of the stage was marked.
147 *nicety* fastidiousness
149 *Vanbrugh and Congreve* Sheridan is mocking himself; he rewrote Vanbrugh's
  The Relapse (1696) and made it much more respectable as *A Trip to
  Scarborough* (1777), besides putting on three Congreve plays, suitably altered,
  at Drury Lane in 1776, his first season as manager.
162-3 *end of the season* See note at I.i.22.

dramatise the penal laws, and make the Stage a court of
ease to the Old Bailey.

DANGLE
It is truly moral.

Enter SERVANT

SERVANT
Sir Fretful Plagiary, Sir.

DANGLE
Beg him to walk up. –   *Exit* SERVANT   175
Now, Mrs Dangle, Sir Fretful Plagiary is an author to your
own taste.

MRS DANGLE
I confess he is a favourite of mine, because everybody else
abuses him.

SNEER
– Very much to the credit of your charity, Madam, if not of   180
your judgment.

DANGLE
But, egad, he allows no merit to any author but himself,
that's the truth on't – though he's my friend.

SNEER
Never. – He is as envious as an old maid verging on the
desperation of six-and-thirty: and then the insidious   185
humility with which he seduces you to give a free opinion
on any of his works, can be exceeded only by the petulant
arrogance with which he is sure to reject your observations.

DANGLE
Very true, egad – though he's my friend.

SNEER
Then his affected contempt of all newspaper strictures;   190

---

173 *It . . . moral.* 1781 (That is to unite [write *deleted*] Poetry and Justice indeed. L)

171-2 *court of ease* The term 'chapel of ease' is used to designate a place of worship
   for the use of parishioners living at a distance from the parish church; here there
   is the same idea but in legal terms. The audience would be acutely aware of the
   difference between the moralising dramatisation of the Old Bailey described
   here and the irreverent treatment of such matters in, for instance, *The Beggar's
   Opera.*
174 *Sir Fretful Plagiary* Sir Fretful is a caricature portrait of the dramatist Richard
   Cumberland (1732–1811), who wrote a number of sentimental comedies as
   well as tragedies. He had in fact a longer active writing life than that of any
   other English playwright (see p. xi).
186 *free* honest, free of partiality

ACT I

though, at the same time, he is the sorest man alive, and
shrinks like scorched parchment from the fiery ordeal of
true criticism: yet is he so covetous of popularity, that he
had rather be abused than not mentioned at all.

DANGLE
There's no denying it – though he is my friend.   195

SNEER
You have read the tragedy he has just finished, haven't you?

DANGLE
O yes; he sent it to me yesterday.

SNEER
Well, and you think it execrable, don't you?

DANGLE
Why between ourselves, egad I must own – though he's my
friend – that it is one of the most – (*aside*) He's here –   200
finished and most admirable perform –

SIR FRETFUL (*without*)
Mr Sneer with him, did you say?

Enter SIR FRETFUL

DANGLE
Ah, my dear friend! – Egad, we were just speaking of your
Tragedy. – Admirable, Sir Fretful, admirable!

SNEER
You never did anything beyond it, Sir Fretful – never in   205
your life.

SIR FRETFUL
You make me extremely happy; – for without a compliment, my dear Sneer, there isn't a man in the world whose
judgment I value as I do yours. – And Mr Dangle's.

MRS DANGLE
They are only laughing at you, Sir Fretful; for it was but   210
just now that –

DANGLE
Mrs Dangle! – Ah, Sir Fretful, you know Mrs Dangle. – My

193–4 *yet . . . all.* 1781 (*omits* L)
200–1 *He's . . . perform* – 1781 (*these lines transferred to follow line 215* L)

200–1 *He's . . . perfor* – These words are slightly differently placed in L, no doubt
    because in the actual performance this seemed better. In the L reading, it may
    have been difficult for Sir Fretful, offstage, to interrupt Dangle at precisely the
    right moment.
207–8 *without a compliment* without any flattery

friend Sneer was rallying just now – He knows how she admires you, and –

SIR FRETFUL
O Lord – I am sure Mr Sneer has more taste and sincerity 215
than to – (*aside*) A damned double-faced fellow!

DANGLE
Yes, yes, – Sneer will jest – but a better humoured –

SIR FRETFUL
O, I know –

DANGLE
He has a ready turn for ridicule – his wit costs him
nothing.   220

SIR FRETFUL (*aside*)
No, egad – or I should wonder how he came by it.

MRS DANGLE
Because his jest is always at the expense of his friend.

DANGLE
But, Sir Fretful, have you sent your play to the managers
yet? – or can I be of any service to you?

SIR FRETFUL
No, no, I thank you; I believe the piece had sufficient 225
recommendation with it. – I thank you though. – I sent it to
the manager of COVENT GARDEN THEATRE this morning.

SNEER
I should have thought now, that it might have been cast (as
the actors call it) better at DRURY LANE.

SIR FRETFUL
O lud! no – never send a play there while I live – 230
harkee! (*whispers [to] SNEER*)

SNEER
Writes himself! – I know he does –

SIR FRETFUL
I say nothing – I take away from no man's merit – am hurt

---

222 *Because ... is* 1781 (Aye the reason is, because his Jests are L)
225 *no, I* ed. (No, I 1781, L)
229 *LANE.* ed. (LANE 1781; Lane. L)

---

213 *rallying* bantering
226 *recommendation* so as not to need Dangle's 'solicited solicitations' (I.i.120)
227 *manager ... THEATRE* Thomas Harris was the manager of Covent Garden, the
chief rival to Drury Lane, from 1767 to 1809. It was he who suggested Sheridan
should write *The Rivals*, which was staged at Covent Garden in 1775. When
Sheridan became manager of Drury Lane in 1776 he and Harris between them
had the monopoly of theatrical power and patronage in London.
228 *cast* provided with performers

at no man's good fortune – I say nothing. – But this I will
say – through all my knowledge of life, I have obser-   235
ved – that there is not a passion so strongly rooted in the
human heart as envy!

SNEER
I believe you have reason for what you say, indeed.

SIR FRETFUL
Besides – I can tell you it is not always so safe to leave a
play in the hands of those who write themselves.   240

SNEER
What, they may steal from them, hey, my dear Plagiary?

SIR FRETFUL
Steal! – to be sure they may; and, egad, serve your best
thoughts as gypsies do stolen children, disfigure them to
make 'em pass for their own.

SNEER
But your present work is a sacrifice to Melpomene, and HE,   245
you know, never –

SIR FRETFUL
That's no security. – A dexterous plagiarist may do anything. – Why, Sir, for aught I know, he might take out some
of the best things in my tragedy, and put them into his own
comedy.   250

SNEER
That might be done, I dare be sworn.

242 *be sure* L (besure 1781)
243 *disfigure* 1781 (disguise [*last two syllables of* disfigure *deleted and* guise *written above*] L)
245-6 HE, *you know, never* 1781 (*omits* L)

238 *you have reason* It being Sir Fretful's own ruling passion.
243 *disfigure them* As the textual note records, the word settled on in L was 'disguise'; Sheridan here gives the common story about gypsies in its more sinister form.
245-6 *and* HE, *you know* Sir Fretful's present play is a sacrifice to the muse of tragedy, and Sheridan, we know, only wrote comedy. The joke is made clearer in 1781 than it was in L.
251 *That might be done* More easily than Sir Fretful supposes: cf. *The Rehearsal* Prol. 13-14: 'Our Poets make us laugh / at Tragedy, / And with their Comedies they make us cry'. Michael Kelly (?1764–1826), later Sheridan's director of music at Drury Lane, tells in his *Reminiscences* the well-known story of Cumberland trying to prevent his children laughing during a performance of *The School for Scandal*, and of Sheridan's response, echoed here: 'It was very ungrateful in Cumberland to have been displeased with his poor children, for laughing at *my comedy*, for I went the other night to see *his tragedy* and laughed at it from beginning to end'.

SIR FRETFUL
    And then, if such a person gives you the least hint or
    assistance, he is devilish apt to take the merit of the
    whole. –
DANGLE
    If it succeeds.   255
SIR FRETFUL
    Aye – but with regard to this piece, I think I can hit that
    gentleman, for I can safely swear he never read it.
SNEER
    I'll tell you how you may hurt him more –
SIR FRETFUL
    How? –
SNEER
    Swear he wrote it.   260
SIR FRETFUL
    Plague on't now, Sneer, I shall take it ill. – I believe you
    want to take away my character as an author!
SNEER
    Then I am sure you ought to be very much obliged to me.
SIR FRETFUL
    Hey! – Sir! –
DANGLE
    O you know, he never means what he says.   265
SIR FRETFUL
    Sincerely then – you do like the piece?
SNEER
    Wonderfully!
SIR FRETFUL
    But come now, there must be something that you think
    might be mended, hey? – Mr Dangle, has nothing struck
    you?   270
DANGLE
    Why faith, it is but an ungracious thing for the most part
    to –
SIR FRETFUL
    – With most authors it is just so indeed; they are in general

---

264–6 *Hey!* . . . *then* – 1781 (*Sir Fretful:* Pshaw now! – but sincerely L)

256–7 *hit that gentleman* get the better of him (i.e. Sheridan)
262 *character* reputation
263 *very much obliged* Sir Fretful uses 'character' in the sense of 'good name'; Sneer
    refers, more damagingly, to Sir Fretful's known reputation as a writer.
269 *mended* improved

strangely tenacious! – But, for my part, I am never so well
pleased as when a judicious critic points out any defect to   275
me; for what is the purpose of showing a work to a friend, if
you don't mean to profit by his opinion?

SNEER
Very true. – Why then, though I seriously admire the piece
upon the whole, yet there is one small objection; which, if
you'll give me leave, I'll mention.   280

SIR FRETFUL
SIR, you can't oblige me more.

SNEER
I think it wants incident.

SIR FRETFUL
Good God! – you surprise me! – wants incident! –

SNEER
Yes; I own I think the incidents are too few.

SIR FRETFUL
Good God! – Believe me, Mr Sneer, there is no person for   285
whose judgment I have a more implicit deference. – But I
protest to you, Mr Sneer, I am only apprehensive that the
incidents are too crowded. – My dear Dangle, how does it
strike you?

DANGLE
Really I can't agree with my friend Sneer. – I think the plot 290
quite sufficient; and the four first acts by many degrees the
best I ever read or saw in my life. If I might venture to
suggest anything, it is that the interest rather falls off in the
fifth. –

SIR FRETFUL
– Rises; I believe you mean, Sir.   295

DANGLE
No; I don't upon my word.

285 *Good... Sneer,* 1781 (Believe me, L)
287 *Mr Sneer,* 1781 (*omits* L)
288 *My dear Dangle,* 1781 (Mr Dangle L)
290 *my friend Sneer* 1781 (Mr Sneer L)

274 *strangely tenacious* Of their own ideas. The obsessive pride and fear of criticism
   of authors was a byword.
285 *Good God!... Sneer* The text of L is less emphatic at this point; the later
   version of the play often embodies minor changes in the way characters are
   addressed, no doubt the result of the experience of what seemed most natural in
   an actual production.
286 *implicit* deep-rooted

SIR FRETFUL
  Yes, yes, you do upon my soul – it certainly don't fall off, I
  assure you – No, no, it don't fall off.
DANGLE
  Now, Mrs Dangle, didn't you say it struck you in the same
  light?   300
MRS DANGLE
  No, indeed, I did not – I did not see a fault in any part of
  the play from the beginning to the end.
SIR FRETFUL
  Upon my soul the women are the best judges after all!
MRS DANGLE
  Or if I made any objection, I am sure it was to nothing in
  the piece; but that I was afraid it was, on the whole, a little   305
  too long.
SIR FRETFUL
  Pray, Madam, do you speak as to duration of time; or do
  you mean that the story is tediously spun out?
MRS DANGLE
  O Lud! no. – I speak only with reference to the usual length
  of acting plays.   310
SIR FRETFUL
  Then I am very happy – very happy indeed, – because the
  play is a short play, a remarkably short play: – I should not
  venture to differ with a lady on a point of taste; but, on
  these occasions, the watch, you know, is the critic.
MRS DANGLE
  Then, I suppose, it must have been Mr Dangle's drawling   315
  manner of reading it to me.
SIR FRETFUL
  O, if Mr Dangle read it! that's quite another affair! – But I
  assure you, Mrs Dangle, the first evening you can spare me
  three hours and a half, I'll undertake to read you the whole

297 *upon my soul* 1781 (*omits* L)
319 *and a half* 1781 (*omits* L)

319–20 *three . . . end* The play is intolerably long, longer than the two and a half
  hours of *The Critic*, itself thought long for an afterpiece (*Morning Chronicle* 1
  November 1779, and see note at II.ii.475–6), longer by half an hour than it was
  in L (see also textual note to line 319). George Sigmond, in the *Memoir* of
  Sheridan prefixed to his 1848 edition of the plays, retells Michael Kelly's story
  of how he and John Bannister (1760–1836: Whiskerandos) were invited by
  Cumberland to his house in Tunbridge Wells and there obliged to hear him
  reading through a play of his in manuscript called *Tiberius*.

from beginning to end, with the Prologue and Epilogue, 320
and allow time for the music between the acts.

MRS DANGLE

I hope to see it on the stage next.

DANGLE

Well, Sir Fretful, I wish you may be able to get rid as easily
of the newspaper criticisms as you do of ours. –

SIR FRETFUL

The NEWSPAPERS! – Sir, they are the most villainous – 325
licentious – abominable – infernal – Not that I ever read
them – No – I make it a rule never to look into a newspaper.

DANGLE

You are quite right – for it certainly must hurt an author of
delicate feelings to see the liberties they take.

SIR FRETFUL

No! – quite the contrary; – their abuse is, in fact, the best 330
panegyric – I like it of all things. – An author's reputation is
only in danger from their support.

SNEER

Why that's true – and that attack now on you the other
day –

SIR FRETFUL

– What? where?   335

DANGLE

Aye, you mean in a paper of Thursday; it was completely
ill-natured to be sure.

SIR FRETFUL

O, so much the better. – Ha! ha! ha! – I wouldn't have it
otherwise.

329 *take.* L (take 1781)
330 *No!* 1781 (O Lud! no L)

---

329 *music between the acts* It was the custom to intersperse even the most solemn
plays with entr'acte songs, dances, processions and pageants. There is a great
deal of dancing in Bayes' play. As he says, 'you must ever interlard your Playes
with Songs, Ghosts, and Dances' (*The Rehearsal* III.i.123–4).

327 *make it a rule* The mention of rules here and elsewhere in the play would
instantly remind the audience of Bayes' rules for writing in *The Rehearsal*
(I.i.94, II.iii.15). The joke is introduced more frequently in 1781 than in L; it
obviously went down well.

331 *panegyric* laudatory judgement

338 *Ha! ha! ha!* Bayes, too, resorts characteristically to this phrase when speaking of
attacks upon himself (e.g. *The Rehearsal* II.ii.30–3).

DANGLE

   Certainly it is only to be laughed at; for –   340

SIR FRETFUL

   – You don't happen to recollect what the fellow said, do
you?

SNEER

   Pray, Dangle – Sir Fretful seems a little anxious –

SIR FRETFUL

   O lud, no! – anxious, – not I, – not the least. – I – But one
may as well hear you know.   345

DANGLE

   Sneer, do *you* recollect? – (*aside*) Make out something.

SNEER (*to* DANGLE)

   I will. – Yes, yes, I remember perfectly.

SIR FRETFUL

   Well, and pray now – Not that it signifies – what might the
gentleman say?

SNEER

   Why, he roundly asserts that you have not the slightest   350
invention, or original genius whatever; though you are the
greatest traducer of all other authors living.

SIR FRETFUL

   Ha! ha! ha! – very good!

SNEER

   That as to COMEDY, you have not one idea of your own, he
believes, even in your commonplace book – where stray   355
jokes, and pilfered witticisms are kept with as much
method as the ledger of the LOST-and-STOLEN OFFICE.

340 *Certainly it is* 1781 (O, It's L)
   for – 1781 (for – certainly what Sir Fretful observes is Extreemly true, an
Author of Eminence who is a candidate for fame ought to distrust – *Sir Fretful:*
It wasn't in the Morning Post, I do sometimes see that. *Dangle:* No, I think
not – I say he ought to distrust his own Merit, if it doesn't create Envy
Sufficient – *Sir Fretful:* Nor the Morning Chronicle – I happen'd to have met
with that lately – *Dangle:* No, I'm sure not – Envy Sufficient I say, to procure
him the sanction of abuse from bad writers. *Sir Fretful:* The Gazetteer – *Dangle:*
I really didn't take notice, as I knew you only laugh'd at these Things. – therefore Mr Sneer, a Man of Sense – L)
347 *will.* (will, 1781; will L)

340 *for*- The joke was more heavy-handed in L.
348 *signifies*   is significant
352 *traducer*   slanderer
355 *commonplace book* Bayes' rules for writing necessitate a 'book of *Drama
Common places*' (*The Rehearsal* I.i.84–5).

SIR FRETFUL
    – Ha! ha! ha! – very pleasant!

SNEER
    Nay, that you are so unlucky as not to have the skill even to
    steal with taste. – But that you glean from the refuse of   360
    obscure volumes, where more judicious plagiarists have
    been before you; so that the body of your work is a
    composition of dregs and sediments – like a bad tavern's
    worst wine.

SIR FRETFUL
    Ha! ha!   365

SNEER
    In your more serious efforts, he says, your bombast would
    be less intolerable, if the thoughts were ever suited to the
    expression; but the homeliness of the sentiment stares
    through the fantastic encumbrance of its fine language, like
    a clown in one of the new uniforms!   370

SIR FRETFUL
    Ha! ha!

SNEER
    That your occasional tropes and flowers suit the general
    coarseness of your style, as tambour sprigs would a
    ground of linsey-wolsey; while your imitations of Shakes-
    peare resemble the mimicry of Falstaff's Page, and are   375
    about as near the standard of the original.

SIR FRETFUL
    Ha! –

SNEER
    – In short, that even the finest passages you steal are of no
    service to you; for the poverty of your own language

---

358 – *very pleasant!* 1781 (*omits* L)
369 *its* ed. (it's 1781, L)

---

370 *clown . . . uniforms* Perhaps for the 1779/80 season Drury Lane had new
    costumes for its clowns.
372 *tropes and flowers*   uses of figurative language
373 *tambour sprigs* Sprays of flowers delicately embroidered using a circular frame
    or tambour; the material so worked would normally not be linsey-wolsey, a
    coarse wool and cotton mixture.
375 *mimicry of Falstaff's Page* The page Prince Hal presented to Falstaff (*2 Henry
    IV* I.ii), who is ludicrously out of proportion to his master.

prevents their assimilating; so that they lie on the surface   380
like lumps of marl on a barren moor, encumbering what it
is not in their power to fertilize! –

SIR FRETFUL (*after great agitation*)
– Now another person would be vexed at this.

SNEER
Oh! but I wouldn't have told you, only to divert you.

SIR FRETFUL
I know it – I *am* diverted, – Ha! ha! ha! – not the least   385
invention! – Ha! ha! ha! very good! – very good!

SNEER
Yes – no genius! Ha! ha! ha!

DANGLE
A severe rogue! Ha! ha! ha! But you are quite right, Sir
Fretful, never to read such nonsense.

SIR FRETFUL
To be sure – for if there is anything to one's praise, it is a   390
foolish vanity to be gratified at it, and if it is abuse, – why
one is always sure to hear of it from one damned good
natured friend or another!

Enter SERVANT

SERVANT
Sir, there is an Italian gentleman, with a French Interpreter, and three young ladies, and a dozen musicians, who   395
say they are sent by LADY RONDEAU and MRS FUGE.

DANGLE
Gadso! they come by appointment. Dear Mrs Dangle do let
them know I'll see them directly.

MRS DANGLE
You know, Mr Dangle, I shan't understand a word they say.

DANGLE
But you hear there's an interpreter.   400

MRS DANGLE
Well, I'll try to endure their complaisance till you come.

Exit

---

386 *very good! – very good!* 1781 (very good. – L)

---

381 *marl* Fertilizer consisting of clay and carbonate of lime. Sir Fretful's plays are
    here the barren moor and the fine passages the useless fertilizer. Contrast
    Falstaff, who is not only witty but 'the cause that wit is in other men' (*2 Henry
    IV* I.ii.11–12).
388 *severe rogue* The modern equivalent might be 'a pretty hard-hitting chap!'
401 *complaisance* politeness, attempts at being agreeable

SERVANT
>And Mr PUFF, Sir, has sent word that the last rehearsal is to
>be this morning, and that he'll call on you presently.

DANGLE
>That's true – I shall certainly be at home.

>*Exit* SERVANT

>Now, Sir Fretful, if you have a mind to have justice done   405
>you in the way of answer – Egad, Mr PUFF's your man.

SIR FRETFUL
>Pshaw! Sir, why should I wish to have it answered, when I
>tell you I am pleased at it?

DANGLE
>True, I had forgot that. – But I hope you are not fretted at
>what Mr Sneer –   410

SIR FRETFUL
>– Zounds! no, Mr Dangle, don't I tell you these things
>never fret me in the least.

DANGLE
>Nay, I only thought –

SIR FRETFUL
>– And let me tell you, Mr Dangle, 'tis damned affronting in
>you to suppose that I am hurt, when I tell you I am not.   415

SNEER
>But why so warm, Sir Fretful?

SIR FRETFUL
>Gadslife! Mr Sneer, you are as absurd as Dangle; how often
>must I repeat it to you, that nothing can vex me but your
>supposing it possible for me to mind the damned nonsense
>you have been repeating to me! – and let me tell you, if you   420
>continue to believe this, you must mean to insult me,
>gentlemen – and then your disrespect will affect me no
>more than the newspaper criticisms – and I shall treat
>it – with exactly the same calm indifference and philosophic
>contempt – and so your servant.   *Exit*   425

SNEER
>Ha! ha! ha! Poor Sir Fretful! Now will he go and vent his
>philosophy in anonymous abuse of all modern critics and
>authors – But, Dangle, you must get your friend PUFF to
>take me to the rehearsal of his tragedy.

DANGLE
>I'll answer for't, he'll thank you for desiring it. But come   430
>and help me to judge of this musical family; they are
>recommended by people of consequence, I assure you.

SNEER

I am at your disposal the whole morning – but I thought
you had been a decided critic in music, as well as in
literature?   435

DANGLE

So I am – but I have a bad ear. – Ifaith, Sneer, though, I am
afraid we were a little too severe on Sir Fretful – though he
is my friend.

SNEER

Why, 'tis certain, that unnecessarily to mortify the vanity
of any writer, is a cruelty which mere dullness never can   440
deserve; but where a base and personal malignity usurps
the place of literary emulation, the aggressor deserves
neither quarter nor pity.

DANGLE

That's true egad! – though he's my friend!

[*Exeunt*]

Act I, Scene ii

A drawing room, harpsichord, &c. Italian family, French
interpreter, MRS DANGLE *and servants discovered*

INTERPRETER

Je dis madame, j'ai l'honneur to *introduce* et de vous
demander votre protection pour le Signor PASTICCIO
RITORNELLO et pour sa charmante famille.

433-6 *but...ear.* 1781 (*omits* L)
  1 *j'ai* (ja'i 1781; J'ai L)
  3 *RITORNELLO* (RETORNELLO 1781; Ritornello L)

437-8 *though...friend* On previous occasions this phrase has suggested that one
   really ought not to criticise one's friends severely; here more cynically it
   suggests that one's friends are precisely the people one says the nastiest things
   about.
439-43 *Why, 'tis certain...pity* – Sneer's speech seems tonally a little out of his
   usual character; it has a directly authorial ring about it.
442 *literary emulation* the striving for literary excellence
  2-3 *PASTICCIO RITORNELLO* The name is significant. A 'pasticcio' is a kind of pie,
   or figuratively a mess or a bungle. It is also a musical term for a composition
   made up from various sources, a pastiche. A 'ritornello' is a refrain or a jingle.

SIGNOR PASTICCIO
Ah! Vosignoria noi vi preghiamo di favoritevi colla vostra
protezione.   5
1ST DAUGHTER
Vosignoria fatevi questi grazzie.
2ND DAUGHTER
Si Signora.
INTERPRETER
Madame – *me interpret.* – C'est à dire – in English – qu'ils
vous prient de leur faire l'honneur –
MRS DANGLE
– I say again, gentlemen, I don't understand a word you say.   10
SIGNOR PASTICCIO
Questo Signore spiegheró.
INTERPRETER
Oui – *me interpret.* – nouse avons les lettres de recommen-
dation pour Monsieur Dangle de –
MRS DANGLE
– Upon my word, Sir, I don't understand you.
SIGNOR PASTICCIO
La CONTESSA RONDEAU e nostra padrona.   15
3RD DAUGHTER
Si, padre, e mi LADI FUGE.
INTERPRETER
O! – *me interpret.* – Madame, ils disent – in English – Qu'ils
ont l'honneur d'être protégés de ces Dames. – *You
understand?*
MRS DANGLE
No, Sir, – no understand!   20

Enter DANGLE *and* SNEER

18 *Dames* ed. (Demes 1781; demes L)

4-5 *Vosignoria...protezione* Sheridan's Italian, even when he is trying to
represent the speech of genuine Italians rather than Dangle's inadequate grasp,
is far from perfect, and has to be rewritten to be the genuine article. No doubt in
the performance by the Italian actor Carlo Antonio Delpini (1740–1828),
Signor Pasticcio would actually have said something like: 'Noi preghiamo
Vossignoria di favorirci della Sua protezione'.
6 *Vosignoria...grazzie* Delpini might have suggested to the English actress
playing his first daughter that she should say: Vossignoria vorrà farci questa
grazia'.
7 *Si* for 'Sì' (as also at line 16)
11 *spiegheró* for 'spiegherà'
15 *e nostra* for 'è la nostra'
16 *mi LADI* for 'MILADY'

INTERPRETER
  Ah voici Monsieur Dangle!
ITALIANS [*together*]
  A! Signor Dangle!
MRS DANGLE
  Mr Dangle, here are two very civil gentlemen trying to
  make themselves understood, and I don't know which is the
  interpreter.   25
DANGLE
  Eh bien!

  [INTERPRETER *and* SIGNOR PASTICCIO] *speaking together*

INTERPRETER
  Monsieur Dangle – le grand bruit de vos talents pour la
  critique et de votre intérêt avec Messieurs les Directeurs à
  tous les Théâtres.
SIGNOR PASTICCIO
  Vosignoria siete si famoso par la vostra conoscensa e vostra   30
  interessa colla le Direttore da –
DANGLE
  Egad I think the Interpreter is the hardest to be understood
  of the two!
SNEER
  Why I thought, Dangle, you had been an admirable linguist!
DANGLE
  So I am, if they would not talk so damned fast.   35
SNEER
  Well I'll explain that – the less time we lose in hearing them

---

23 *Mr Dangle* 1781 (My Dear L)
31 *da* – 1781 (ti both Theatre L)
34–46 *linguist! ... room.* 1781 (Linguist, I am sure you write the Account of
   foreign Literature in one of the Reviews. *Dangle:* Yes, but it is not necessary to
   understand the Languages for that, Why reading the Books is mere
   Journeymans Work, I get that done by the Sheet, and so Skim over a
   Translation in Abstract. L)

30–1 *Vosignoria ... da* – for 'Vossignoria è così famoso per le Sue conoscenze e il
   Suo interesse presso i Direttori dei –'
34 *admirable linguist* Dangle's inadequate grasp of foreign languages, which he
   admits to in L, rather than enacting it, as in 1781, reminds us of Bayes in *The
   Rehearsal* (I.i.195–200), and of his sense that speaking French shows breeding
   (II.ii.17–18).

the better, – for that I suppose is what they are brought here
for.

SNEER *speaks to* SIGNOR PASTICCIO. *They sing trios, &c.,*
DANGLE *beating out of time.* SERVANT *enters and whispers* [*to*]
DANGLE

DANGLE
 Show him up.   *Exit* SERVANT
 Bravo! admirable! bravissimo! admirablissimo! – Ah! Sneer!   40
 where will you find such as these voices in England?
SNEER
 Not easily.
DANGLE
 But PUFF is coming. – Signor and little Signoras – obligatis-
 simo! – Sposa Signora Danglena – Mrs Dangle, shall I beg
 you to offer them some refreshments, and take their   45
 address in the next room.
                      Exit MRS DANGLE *with the* ITALIANS
                           and INTERPRETER *ceremoniously*

                    Enter SERVANT

SERVANT
 Mr PUFF, Sir!
DANGLE
 My dear PUFF!

                    Enter PUFF

PUFF
 My dear Dangle, how is it with you?
DANGLE
 Mr Sneer, give me leave to introduce Mr PUFF to you.   50
PUFF
 Mr Sneer is this? Sir, he is a gentleman whom I have long
 panted for the honour of knowing – a gentleman whose
 critical talents and transcendent judgment –
SNEER
 – Dear Sir –

---

51 *is this* 1781 (*omits* L)

---

38 sd *sing trios* In the early performances the trio sung here was in French, sung by
    Carlo Delpini, Ann Field (?–1789) and one of the Miss Abrams, no doubt
    Harriet (1760–?1825), with a duet following it in Italian sung by Miss Field and
    Miss Abrams. Dangle beats out of time just as Bayes clumsily joins in with his
    own actors (*The Rehearsal* III.v.84–5; III.v.146 sd; V.i.89 sd; V.i.328 sd).

DANGLE

Nay, don't be modest, Sneer; my friend PUFF only talks to   55
you in the style of his profession.

SNEER

His profession!

PUFF

Yes, Sir; I make no secret of the trade I follow – among
friends and brother authors, Dangle knows I love to be
frank on the subject, and to advertise myself *viva voce*. – I   60
am, Sir, a Practitioner in Panegyric, or to speak more
plainly – a Professor of the Art of Puffing, at your
service – or anybody else's.

SNEER

Sir, you are very obliging! – I believe, Mr Puff, I have often
admired your talents in the daily prints.   65

PUFF

Yes, Sir, I flatter myself I do as much business in that way
as any six of the fraternity in town – Devilish hard work all
the summer – Friend Dangle? never worked harder! – But
harkee, – the Winter Managers were a little sore I believe.

DANGLE

No – I believe they took it all in good part.   70

PUFF

Ah! – Then that must have been affectation in them, for
egad, there were some of the attacks which there was no
laughing at!

SNEER

Aye, the humorous ones. – But I should think Mr Puff, that
Authors would in general be able to do this sort of work for   75
themselves.

PUFF

Why yes – but in a clumsy way. – Besides, we look on that
as an encroachment, and so take the opposite side. – I dare
say now you conceive half the very civil paragraphs and
advertisements you see to be written by the parties   80
concerned, or their friends? – No such thing – Nine out of
ten manufactured by me in the way of business.

SNEER

Indeed! –

71 *Ah* L (Aye 1781)

---

60 *viva voce* aloud, without disguise
65 *prints* newspapers
67 *fraternity* fellow practitioners
69 *the Winter Managers* See note at I.i.22.

PUFF

Even the Auctioneers now, – the Auctioneers I say, though
the rogues have lately got some credit for their language   85
– not an article of the merit theirs! – take them out of their
Pulpits, and they are as dull as Catalogues. – No,
Sir; – 'twas I first enriched their style – 'twas I first taught
them to crowd their advertisements with panegyrical
superlatives, each epithet rising above the other – like the   90
Bidders in their own Auction rooms! From ME they learnt
to inlay their phraseology with variegated chips of exotic
metaphor: by ME too their inventive faculties were called
forth. – Yes Sir, by ME they were instructed to clothe ideal
walls with gratuitous fruits – to insinuate obsequious rivu-   95
lets into visionary groves – to teach courteous shrubs to nod
their approbation of the grateful soil! or on emergencies to
raise upstart oaks, where there never had been an acorn; to
create a delightful vicinage without the assistance of a
neighbour; or fix the temple of Hygeia in the fens of   100
Lincolnshire!

DANGLE

I am sure you have done them infinite service; for now,
when a gentleman is ruined, he parts with his house with
some credit.

SNEER

Service! if they had any gratitude, they would erect a statue   105
to him, they would figure him as a presiding Mercury, the
god of traffic and fiction, with a hammer in his hand instead
of a caduceus. – But pray, Mr Puff, what first put you on
exercising your talents in this way?

85 *credit for their language* The language used by auctioneers to recommend houses
to prospective buyers went, then as now, beyond the cataloguing of sober detail.
The style in which auctions were advertised in the *Morning Post*, especially, was
very superior.

92-3 *inlay...metaphor* like a kind of linguistic marquetry

95 *gratuitous* free and abundant, not laboured for

99 *vicinage* neighbourhood

100-1 *Hygeia...Lincolnshire* Lincolnshire was notoriously damp and unhealthy,
hardly the place for a temple to the goddess of health. The reference may be a
hit at the quack doctor James Graham (1745-94), who opened a very elaborate
establishment he called 'The Temple of Health' in London in the autumn of
1779.

106-8 *Mercury...caduceus* Mercury, the messenger of the gods and patron of
travellers and of persuasive orators, carried the caduceus, a rod entwined at one
end by two serpents, which he had been given by Apollo.

PUFF

Egad Sir, – sheer necessity – the proper parent of an art so   110
nearly allied to invention: you must know Mr Sneer, that
from the first time I tried my hand at an advertisement, my
success was such, that for some time after, I led a most
extraordinary life indeed!

SNEER

How, pray?   115

PUFF

Sir, I supported myself two years entirely by my misfortunes.

SNEER

By your misfortunes!

PUFF

Yes Sir, assisted by long sickness, and other occasional
disorders; and a very comfortable living I had of it.   120

SNEER

From sickness and misfortunes! – You practised as a
Doctor, and an Attorney at once?

PUFF

No egad, both maladies and miseries were my own.

SNEER

Hey! – what the plague!

DANGLE

'Tis true, ifaith.   125

PUFF

Harkee! – By advertisements – 'To the charitable and humane!' and 'to those whom Providence hath blessed with
affluence!'

SNEER

Oh, – I understand you.

PUFF

And in truth, I deserved what I got, for I suppose never   130
man went through such a series of calamities in the same
space of time! – Sir, I was five times made a bankrupt, and
reduced from a state of affluence, by a train of unavoidable
misfortunes! then Sir, though a very industrious tradesman,
I was twice burnt out, and lost my little all, both   135

110–11 *necessity...invention* Puff's reference is to the proverbial saying that
'necessity is the mother of invention'.

135 *twice burnt out* Fires in the poorer parts of eighteenth-century London, where
many buildings were of wood and where there were many illicit stills, were
frequent and terrible.

times! – I lived upon those fires a month. – I soon after was confined by a most excruciating disorder, and lost the use of my limbs! – That told very well, for I had the case strongly attested, and went about to collect the subscriptions myself. 140

DANGLE
Egad, I believe that was when you first called on me. –

PUFF
– In November last? – O no! – I was at that time a close prisoner in the Marshalsea, for a debt benevolently contracted to serve a friend! – I was afterwards twice tapped for a dropsy, which declined into a very profitable 145 consumption! – I was then reduced to – O no – then I became a widow with six helpless children, – after having had eleven husbands pressed, and being left every time eight months gone with child, and without money to get me into an hospital! 150

SNEER
And you bore all with patience, I make no doubt?

PUFF
Why, yes, – though I made some occasional attempts at felo de se; but as I did not find those *rash actions* answer, I left off killing myself very soon. – Well, Sir, – at last, what with bankruptcies, fires, gouts, dropsies, imprisonments, and 155 other valuable calamities, having got together a pretty handsome sum, I determined to quit a business which had always gone rather against my conscience, and in a more liberal way still to indulge my talents for fiction and embellishment, through my favourite channels of diurnal 160 communication – and so, Sir, you have my history.

143 *Marshalsea* the debtors' prison on the south bank of the Thames
145 *tapped for a dropsy* The watery fluid collecting in the body tissues of a patient suffering from dropsy has to be drained off.
148 *pressed* press-ganged into the navy
152–3 *felo de se* suicide
160–1 *channels of diurnal communication* daily newspapers

SNEER

Most obligingly communicative indeed; and your confes-
sion if published, might certainly serve the cause of true
charity, by rescuing the most useful channels of appeal to
benevolence from the cant of imposition. – But surely, Mr   165
PUFF, there is no great *mystery* in your present profession?

PUFF

Mystery! Sir, I will take upon me to say the matter was
never scientifically treated, nor reduced to rule before.

SNEER

Reduced to rule?

PUFF

O lud, Sir! you are very ignorant, I am afraid. – Yes   170
Sir, – PUFFING is of various sorts – the principal are, The
PUFF DIRECT – the PUFF PRELIMINARY – the PUFF COLLA-
TERAL – the PUFF COLLUSIVE, and the PUFF OBLIQUE, or
PUFF by IMPLICATION. – These all assume, as circumstances
require, the various forms of LETTER TO THE EDITOR –   175
OCCASIONAL ANECDOTE – IMPARTIAL CRITIQUE – OBSER-
VATION from CORRESPONDENT, – or ADVERTISEMENT FROM
THE PARTY.

SNEER

The puff direct, I can conceive –

PUFF

O yes, that's simple enough, – for instance – A new Comedy   180

162-5 *and your . . . imposition.* 1781 (*omits* L)
174-5 *as circumstances require,* 1781 (*omits* L)

162-5 *and your . . . imposition* This passage, which does not appear in L, comments
in a suddenly rather acid tone on Puff's deceitful use of the kind of
advertisement often to be seen in newspapers of the time, appealing for
charitable help. The *Morning Chronicle* of 2 November 1779, describing the
successful second performance of the play, nevertheless records that Puff's
ridiculing of 'addresses to the humane and benevolent' was not liked: 'to this a
great part of the audience opposed a long and virtuous hiss'. The report goes on
to say that King as Puff then 'seized a lucky moment' to say a few extra lines
(not in the original play text) to explain that he intended no hit against genuine
advertisements for help; Sheridan in the authorised printed text of 1781 did not
include these impromptu words by Puff (because no doubt they were
awkwardly out of character), but gave the burden of moral comment (still a
little awkwardly out of character) to Sneer.
171-4 *The PUFF . . . IMPLICATION* The echo here is of Touchstone's speech at the end
of *As You Like It* on the way to 'quarrel in print by the book'.
177-8 *FROM THE PARTY* Items of a political kind were regularly inserted in
newspapers in the late eighteenth century, and it seems as though Puff is
referring here to contributions of this sort.

or Farce is to be produced at one of the Theatres (though
by the bye they don't bring out half what they ought to do).
The author, suppose Mr Smatter, or Mr Dapper – or any
particular friend of mine – very well; the day before it is to
be performed, I write an account of the manner in which it   185
was received – I have the plot from the author, – and only
add – Characters strongly drawn – highly coloured – hand
of a master – fund of genuine humour – mine of invention – neat dialogue – attic salt! Then for the performance – Mr Dodd was astonishingly great in the character of   190
Sir Harry! That universal and judicious actor Mr Palmer,
perhaps never appeared to more advantage than in the
Colonel; – but it is not in the power of language to do
justice to Mr King! – Indeed he more than merited those
repeated bursts of applause which he drew from a most   195
brilliant and judicious audience! As to the scenery – The

182 *do).* ed. (do) 1781, L)
183 *Dapper* 1781 (Flimsey L)
193 *not in the power of* 1781 (impossible for L)

---

183 *Mr Dapper* The name Flimsey used in L clearly chimed in unadventurously
    with Sir Flimsy Gossimer, who appears shortly.
189 *attic salt* elegant wit
190–1 *Mr Dodd...Harry* James Dodd (?1740–96), who created the part of
    Dangle, and who, like the other two actors mentioned, is on stage at this
    moment, had recently played Sir Harry Bouquet in Sheridan's musical
    entertainment *The Camp* (1778); but the reference may be to Sir Harry Wildair
    in Farquhar's *The Constant Couple* (1700).
191–3 *Mr Palmer... Colonel* John Palmer (1744–98), as Sneer, listens to praise
    of himself probably as Colonel Standard in *The Constant Couple*. It is worth
    noting that Palmer had played Earl Edwin in Cumberland's *The Battle of
    Hastings* when it was successfully produced at Drury Lane in 1778. Sheridan
    had accepted the play after it had been turned down by Covent Garden.
194 *Mr King* Thomas King (1730–1805), the chief comic actor at Drury Lane, as
    Puff, is of course actually speaking these lines of ecstatic praise of himself, and
    he must have enjoyed the lines, for in 1781 the original phrasing of L at I.ii.193
    is replaced by a phrase which could be slowly relished in the delivery. Sheridan
    is making friendly fun of his own actors and of himself as well, since he too
    wrote puffs for his own theatre in the newspapers. It is pleasant to recall that
    when Thomas King finally quit the stage, at Drury Lane on 24 May 1802, amid
    the affectionate good wishes of audience and fellow players, his last address to
    the public was written by Richard Cumberland. See also note at I.i.112–13.

miraculous power of Mr DE LOUTHERBOURG's pencil is
universally acknowledged! – In short, we are at a loss which
to admire most, – the unrivalled genius of the author, the
great attention and liberality of the managers – the   200
wonderful abilities of the painter, or the incredible
exertions of all the performers! –

SNEER
That's pretty well indeed, Sir.

PUFF
O cool – quite cool – to what I sometimes do.

SNEER
And do you think there are any who are influenced by this?   205

PUFF
O, lud! yes, Sir; – the number of those who go through the
fatigue of judging for themselves is very small indeed!

SNEER
Well, Sir, – The PUFF PRELIMINARY?

PUFF
O that, Sir, does well in the form of a *Caution*. – In a matter
of gallantry now – Sir FLIMSY GOSSIMER wishes to be well   210
with LADY FANNY FETE – He applies to me – I open
trenches for him with a paragraph in the Morning Post. – It
is recommended to the beautiful and accomplished Lady F
four stars F dash E to be on her guard against that
dangerous character, Sir F dash G; who, however pleasing   215
and insinuating his manners may be, is certainly not
remarkable for the *constancy of his attachments!* – in

---

197 DE (DE 1781; *omits* L)
       is (are 1781, L)
205 *this?* L (this. 1781)

---

197 *Mr* DE LOUTHERBOURG Philippe de Loutherbourg (1740–1812), an Alsatian of
       Polish descent, was Garrick's and then Sheridan's scene designer at Drury Lane
       (1771–81). The masque *Alfred* was his first production, in 1773 (see note at
       III.i.288 sd). He was particularly good at romantic and picturesque landscape
       painting, and the realism of his stage effects dazzled audiences in the 1770s. The
       scene with which Puff's tragedy and *The Critic* ends must have been
       particularly impressive (see p. xvi).
199 *genius of the author* Thomas King, as Puff, is the author of the play we are to see
       rehearsed; as manager of Sadler's Wells (1772–82) he probably put together
       The Prophecy; or, Queen Elizabeth at Tilbury, performed with great success in
       June 1779 at the height of the alarm about invasion by France and Spain. The
       puff here also spills over, of course, into praise of *The Critic* itself and of the
       genius who was its author.
211–12 *open trenches* begin the siege

Italics. – Here you see, Sir FLIMSY GOSSIMER is introduced
to the particular notice of Lady FANNY – who perhaps
never thought of him before – she finds herself publicly   220
cautioned to avoid him, which naturally makes her desirous
of seeing him; – the observation of their acquaintance
causes a pretty kind of mutual embarrassment, this
produces a sort of sympathy of interest – which, if Sir
Flimsy is unable to improve effectually, he at least gains   225
the credit of having their names mentioned together, by a
particular set, and in a particular way, – which nine times
out of ten is the full accomplishment of modern gallantry!

DANGLE
Egad, Sneer, you will be quite an adept in the business.

PUFF
Now, Sir, the PUFF COLLATERAL is much used as an   230
appendage to advertisements, and may take the form of
anecdote. – Yesterday as the celebrated GEORGE BON-MOT
was sauntering down St James's street, he met the lively
Lady MARY MYRTLE, coming out of the Park, – 'Good
God, LADY MARY, I'm surprised to meet you in a white   235
jacket, – for I expected never to have seen you, but in a full-
trimmed uniform, and a light-horseman's cap!' – 'Heavens,
GEORGE, where could you have learned that?' – 'Why,'
replied the wit, 'I just saw a print of you, in a new
publication called The CAMP MAGAZINE, which, by the bye,   240
is a devilish clever thing, – and is sold at No. 3, on the right
hand of the way, two doors from the printing office, the
corner of Ivy Lane, Paternoster Row, price only one
shilling!'

SNEER
Very ingenious indeed!   245

PUFF
But the PUFF COLLUSIVE is the newest of any; for it acts in
the disguise of determined hostility. – It is much used by
bold booksellers and enterprising poets. – An indignant

227 *particular set, and in a* 1781 *(omits* L)

232 *GEORGE BON-MOT* George Bon-Mot is clearly George Selwyn, a noted wit;
Boswell, in his London journal for 5 January 1763, calls him 'one of the
brightest geniuses in England, of whom more good sayings are recorded than
anybody'. See note at Prologue: *RICHARD FITZPATRICK.*
240 *The* CAMP *MAGAZINE* See note at I.i.4.

correspondent observes – that the new poem called BEELZE-
BUB'S COTILLION, or PROSERPINE'S FETE CHAMPETRE, is　250
one of the most unjustifiable performances he ever read!
The severity with which certain characters are handled is
quite shocking! And as there are many descriptions in it too
warmly coloured for female delicacy, the shameful avidity
with which this piece is bought by all people of fashion, is a　255
reproach on the taste of the times, and a disgrace to the
delicacy of the age! – Here you see the two strongest
inducements are held forth; – First, that nobody ought to
read it; – and secondly, that everybody buys it; on the
strength of which, the publisher boldly prints the tenth　260
edition, before he has sold ten of the first; and then
establishes it by threatening himself with the pillory, or
absolutely indicating himself for SCAN. MAG!

DANGLE

Ha! ha! ha! – 'gad I know it is so.

PUFF

As to the PUFF OBLIQUE, or PUFF BY IMPLICATION, it is too　265
various and extensive to be illustrated by an instance; – it
attracts in titles, and presumes in patents; it lurks in the
limitation of a subscription, and invites in the assurance of
crowd and incommodation at public places; it delights to
draw forth concealed merit, with a most disinterested　270
assiduity; and sometimes wears a countenance of smiling
censure and tender reproach. – It has a wonderful memory

261　*has* L (had 1781)
269–72　*it ... reproach.* 1781 (*omits* L)

249–50　*BEELZEBUB* the devil
250　*COTILLION* a brisk dance for four or eight people
　　　PROSERPINE queen of the underworld
　　　FETE CHAMPETRE an outdoor entertainment for fashionable people
260　*publisher boldy prints* Chatterton in 1770 commented on the contemporary book
　　　trade in a poem called 'The art of puffing by a bookseller's journeyman'.
263　*SCAN. MAG Scandalum magnatum* (=defamation of magnates), or words in
　　　derogation of the Crown, peers, judges, and other principal officers of the realm,
　　　became a legal offence in the reign of Richard II.
267　*patents* A patent is a government grant of some exclusive privilege.
268　*limitation of a subscription* subscription of money, for a book for instance or a
　　　cause, open only to the select few
269　*incommodation* inconvenience

for Parliamentary Debates, and will often give the whole
speech of a favoured member, with the most flattering
accuracy. But, above all, it is a great dealer in reports and   275
suppositions. – It has the earliest intelligence of intended
preferments that will reflect *honour* on the *patrons*; and
embryo promotions of modest gentlemen – who know
nothing of the matter themselves. It can hint a riband for
implied services, in the air of a common report; and with   280
the carelessness of a casual paragraph suggest officers into
commands – to which they have no pretension but their
wishes. This, Sir, is the last principal class in the ART of
PUFFING – An art which I hope you will now agree with me,
is of the highest dignity – yielding a tablature of benevo-   285
lence and public spirit; befriending equally trade, gallantry,
criticism, and politics: – the applause of genius! the register
of charity! the triumph of heroism! the self-defence of
contractors! the fame of orators! – and the gazette of
ministers!   290

SNEER
Sir, I am completely a convert both to the importance and
ingenuity of your profession; and now, Sir, there is but one
thing which can possibly increase my respect for you, and
that is, your permitting me to be present this morning at the
rehearsal of your new trage –   295

PUFF
– Hush, for heaven's sake. – *My* tragedy! – Egad, Dangle, I
take this very ill – you know how apprehensive I am of
being known to be the author.

DANGLE
Ifaith I would not have told – but it's in the papers, and
your name at length – in the Morning Chronicle.   300

289 *orators* 1781 (Patriots L)

273–4 *whole . . . member* Sheridan was elected an MP in 1780, and became famous
as a Parliamentary speaker. William Woodfall of the *Morning Chronicle* was
known for his accurate reports of debates. See note at I.i.7–8.
278 *embryo promotions* promotions as yet hardly in the realm of the possible
279 *riband* ribbon, decoration
285 *yielding a tablature* giving a graphic picture
287–8 *the register of charity* the way of registering that an act of charity has been
performed
289 *gazette* See note at I.i.9.
296–7 *I take this very ill* Puff's discomfiture is, of course, entirely feigned, since he
has himself leaked the identity of the author to the newspapers.

PUFF

Ah! those damned editors never can keep a secret! – Well,
Mr Sneer – no doubt you will do me great honour – I shall
be infinitely happy – highly flattered –

DANGLE

I believe it must be near the time – shall we go together?

PUFF

No; it will not be yet this hour, for they are always late at   305
that theatre: besides, I must meet you there, for I have
some little matters here to send to the papers, and a few
paragraphs to scribble before I go. (*looking at memoran-
dums*) – Here is 'a CONSCIENTIOUS BAKER, on the Subject of
the Army Bread'; and 'a DETESTER OF VISIBLE BRICKWORK,   310
in favour of the new invented Stucco'; both in the style of
JUNIUS, and promised for tomorrow. – The Thames navigation too is at a stand. – MISOMUD or ANTI-SHOAL must go to
work again directly. – Here too are some political memo-
randums I see; aye – To take PAUL JONES, and get the   315
INDIAMEN out of the SHANNON – reinforce BYRON – compel
the DUTCH to – so! – I must do that in the evening papers,
or reserve it for the Morning Herald, for I know that I have
undertaken tomorrow, besides, to establish the unanimity

---

304 *together?* (together. 1781, L)
305 *it* (It 1781, L)
318 *or ... Herald,* 1781 (*omits* L)
319 *tomorrow,* ed. (to-morrow; 1781; to morrow L)

311–12 *style of JUNIUS* See note at I.i.1. 'Junius' wrote with bitter scorn and
invective, but upon subjects of greater concern than Puff's.

312–13 *Thames navigation* There were complaints in the newspapers at the time
that the Thames was not being properly dredged. Puff's newspaper pseudonym,
'Misomud' (i.e. hater of mud), is of a fashionably classical kind.

315 *PAUL JONES* John Paul Jones (1747–92) was born in Scotland, but joined the
American navy in 1775 and menaced the English coast. In 1779, with a small
force of French and American ships, he threatened Edinburgh.

316 *INDIAMEN out of the SHANNON* We must presume that these merchants ships of
the East India Company had taken refuge in the Shannon from French
privateers of the kind Paul Jones commanded.

BYRON John Byron (1723–86) was commander of the West Indies fleet in
1778–9. Before engaging the French Admiral D'Estaing with a fleet much
damaged by storms, he sailed for St Kitts to secure the safe passage of trade
ships for England (see I.i.3–4). The sugar trade from the West Indies had
absolutely to be safeguarded if there was to be the money and the will to
conduct a war.

of the fleet in the Public Advertiser, and to shoot CHARLES   320
FOX in the Morning Post, – So, egad, I haven't a moment to
lose!

DANGLE
Well! – we'll meet in the Green Room.

                                              Exeunt severally

Act II, Scene i

The Theatre

Enter DANGLE, PUFF, *and* SNEER, *as before the curtain*

PUFF
No, no, Sir; what Shakespeare says of ACTORS may be better
applied to the purpose of PLAYS; *they* ought to be 'the
abstract and brief Chronicles of the times'. Therefore when
history, and particularly the history of our own country,
furnishes anything like a case in point to the time in which   5
an author writes, if he knows his own interest, he will take
advantage of it; so, Sir, I call my tragedy The SPANISH
ARMADA; and have laid the scene before TILBURY FORT.

SNEER
A most happy thought certainly!

320–3 *and to ... Room.* 1781 (and recover three Men for the Humane Society in the
    Morning Post – So egad I haven't a moment – Well we'll meet in the Green
    Room – But Dangle I must beg you not to tell a Word of the Plot, or Characters
    of my Play to our Friend till we meet. *Dangle:* I wont Indeed. *Sneer:* I shall be
    all Impatience *Puff:* Egad I think we shall Surprize him, hey? L)
  1 *No, no, Sir;* 1781 (Sir, I say, that L)

320–1 CHARLES FOX Charles James Fox (1749–1806), a leading Whig opponent of
    George III and Lord North (see note at I.i.1), had become a close friend and
    political ally of Sheridan's in 1780, thus earning a place in *The Critic* (the
    reference does not occur in L), where a number of Sheridan's friends had genial
    fun poked at them. Fox particularly attacked the administration's naval policy
    at this time.
323 *the Green Room* The waiting-room for performers about to go on stage. Such
    rooms were originally painted green to relieve the eyes from the glare of the
    light on the candlelit stage.
  2–3 *the ... times* See note at I.i.82–5.
  7–8 *The SPANISH ARMADA* See note at I.ii.199.
  8 *TILBURY FORT* A fortification that was built in the reign of Henry VIII to defend
    the mouth of the Thames.

DANGLE

Egad it was – I told you so. – But pray now I don't   10
understand how you have contrived to introduce any love
into it.

PUFF

Love! – Oh nothing so easy; for it is a received point among
poets, that where history gives you a good heroic outline for
a play, you may fill up with a little love at your own   15
discretion; in doing which, nine times out of ten, you only
make up a deficiency in the private history of the
times. – Now I rather think I have done this with some
success.

SNEER

No scandal about Queen ELIZABETH, I hope?   20

PUFF

O Lud! no, no. – I only suppose the Governor of Tilbury
Fort's daughter to be in love with the son of the Spanish
Admiral.

SNEER

Oh, is that all?

DANGLE

Excellent, ifaith! – I see it at once. – But won't this appear   25
rather improbable?

PUFF

To be sure it will – but what the plague! a play is not to
show occurrences that happen every day, but things just so
strange, that though they never *did*, they *might* happen.

SNEER

Certainly nothing is unnatural, that is not physically   30
impossible.

PUFF

Very true – and for that matter DON FEROLO WHISKERAN-
DOS – for that's the lover's name, might have been over here

---

10 *don't* (dont 1781, L)
12 *it.* 1781 (it, and that you know is as necessary to a modern Tragedy as – *Sneer:*
    Novelty to a Simile, and therefore you had better not try to make Love on the
    Subject L)
25 *ifaith* (Efaith 1781, L)
32–3 *WHISKERANDOS* ed. (WISKERANDOS 1781; Whiskerondos L)

32–3 *DON FEROLO WHISKERANDOS* As the textual notes show, the final form of this
    name, as it appears in the Dramatis Personae of the 1781 text, was a little slow
    being fixed. See note at II.ii.85.

in the train of the Spanish Ambassador; or TILBURINA, for
that is the lady's name, might have been in love with him   35
from having heard his character, or seen his picture; or
from knowing that he was the last man in the world she
ought to be in love with – or for any other good female
reason. – However, Sir, the fact is, that though she is but a
Knight's daugher, egad! she is in love like any Princess!   40

DANGLE
Poor young lady! I feel for her already! for I can conceive
how great the conflict must be between her passion and her
duty; her love for her country, and her love for DON
FEROLO WHISKERANDOS!

PUFF
O amazing! – her poor susceptible heart is swayed to and fro   45
by contending passions like –

Enter UNDER PROMPTER

UNDER PROMPTER
Sir, the scene is set, and everything is ready to begin if you
please. –

PUFF
Egad; then we'll lose no time.

UNDER PROMPTER
Though I believe, Sir, you will find it very short, for all the   50
performers have profited by the kind permission you
granted them.

PUFF
Hey! what!

UNDER PROMPTER
You know, Sir, you gave them leave to cut out or omit
whatever they found heavy or unnecessary to the plot, and   55
I must own they have taken very liberal advantage of your
indulgence.

---

44 *WHISKERANDOS* ed. (WISKERANDOS 1781; Whiskerondos L)

34 *TILBURINA* the damsel of Tilbury, as it were
43–4 *her love . . . WHISKERANDOS* Cumberland's *The Battle of Hastings* (1778)
introduces a conflict between Edgar's love for Edwina and his duty to his
country, summed up in the memorable line from the first scene: 'For England,
not Edwina, now demands you!' Volscius in *The Rehearsal* suffers a similar
agonising dilemma (III.v.95): 'Go on, cries Honour; tender Love saies, nay'.

PUFF

Well, well. – They are in general very good judges; and I
know I am luxuriant. – [calls out] Now, Mr HOPKINS, as
soon as you please.   60

UNDER PROMPTER (to the music)

Gentlemen, will you play a few bars of something, just to –

PUFF

Aye, that's right, – for as we have the scenes, and dresses,
egad, we'll go to't, as if it was the first night's performance; – but you need not mind stopping between the acts.

Exit UNDER PROMPTER

Orchestra play. Then the bell rings

So! stand clear gentlemen. – Now you know there will be a   65
cry of down! – down! – hats off! silence! – Then up curtain, – and let us see what our painters have done for us.

Act II, Scene ii

The curtain rises and discovers Tilbury Fort
Two sentinels asleep

DANGLE

Tilbury Fort! – very fine indeed!

PUFF

Now, what do you think I open with?

SNEER

Faith, I can't guess –

---

64 *– but . . . acts.* 1781 (*omits* L)

58 *very good judges* The power of the actors combined perhaps with the influence
of others involved in a theatrical production to undermine the primacy of the
play text and so discourage fine plays in the eighteenth century (see note at
II.ii.212); Bayes a hundred years before was also defeated by his actors (*The
Rehearsal* II.ii.33, V.i.392–400).

59 *Mr HOPKINS* William Hopkins (?–1780), prompter and copyist at Drury Lane
from 1760 to 1780. He does not at any point in the play actually appear on
stage, though he does speak at II.ii.455 and III.i.271. His wife, Elizabeth
(1731–1801), played the part of Mrs Dangle. It is interesting to note, too, that
Charles Bannister (1741–1804), the father of John (see note at I.i.314–20), had
played the part of Hopkins the Prompter in Garrick's *A Peep behind the Curtain*
in 1767 (see pp. xii–xiii).

62 *scenes, and dresses* scenery and costumes

1 sd *Two sentinels asleep* a parody of the opening of *Hamlet*

PUFF

A clock. – Hark! – (*clock strikes*) I open with a clock
striking, to beget an awful attention in the audience – it   5
also marks the time, which is four o'clock in the morning,
and saves a description of the rising sun, and a great deal
about gilding the eastern hemisphere.

DANGLE

But pray, are the sentinels to be asleep?

PUFF

Fast as watchmen.   10

SNEER

Isn't that odd though at such an alarming crisis?

PUFF

To be sure it is, – but smaller things must give way to a
striking scene at the opening; that's a rule. – And the case is,
that two great men are coming to this very spot to begin the
piece; now, it is not to be supposed they would open their   15
lips, if these fellows were watching them; so, egad, I must
either have sent them off their posts, or set them asleep.

SNEER

O that accounts for it! – But tell us, who are these
coming? –

PUFF

These are they – SIR WALTER RALEIGH, and SIR CHRISTO-   20
PHER HATTON. – You'll know Sir CHRISTOPHER, by his
turning out his toes – famous you know for his dancing. I
like to preserve all the little traits of character. – Now
attend.

Enter SIR WALTER RALEIGH *and* SIR
CHRISTOPHER HATTON

12 *To be sure it is* 1781 (Aye L)
13 *that's a rule.* 1781 (*omits* L)

---

4 *I open with a clock* Bayes' play begins oddly too, with a whisper (*The Rehearsal*
II.i).
5 *awful* inspiring awe
13 *that's a rule* See note at I.i.327.
20-1 *SIR WALTER RALEIGH, and SIR CHRISTOPHER HATTON* Sir Walter Raleigh
(c.1552–1618), knighted in 1584, later captain of the Queen's Guard, was in
many ways the typical Elizabethan adventurer; Sir Christopher Hatton
(1540–91) was created Lord Chancellor in 1587, the year before the Armada.
George Sigmond comments: 'Mr Waldron, as Sir Christopher Hatton, was more
popular in that short and insignificant character than in any that he performed.
It was said by Sheridan, that he made more points by his toes than by his brains.'

PUFF

Here, now you see, Sir Christopher did not in fact ask any   105
one question for his own information.

SNEER

No indeed: – his has been a most disinterested curiosity!

DANGLE

Really, I find, we are very much obliged to them both.

PUFF

To be sure you are. Now then for the Commander in Chief,
the EARL OF LEICESTER! who, you know, was no favourite   110
but of the Queen's. – [to the actors] We left off – 'in
amazement lost!' –

SIR CHRISTOPHER

Am in amazement lost. –
But see where noble Leicester comes! supreme
In honours and command.

SIR WALTER   *And yet methinks,*   115
At such a time, so perilous, so feared,
That staff might well become an abler grasp.

SIR CHRISTOPHER

And so by heaven! think I; but soft, he's here!

PUFF

Aye, they envy him.

SNEER

But who are these with him?   120

PUFF

O! very valiant knights; one is the Governor of the fort, the
other the master of the horse. – And now, I think you shall
hear some better language: I was obliged to be plain and
intelligible in the first scene, because there was so much
matter of fact in it; but now, ifaith, you have trope, figure,   125
and metaphor, as plenty as noun substantives.

109 *Commander in Chief* 1781 (Generalissimo L)
121–2 *the other . . . horse.* 1781 (*omits* L)

---

110 *EARL OF LEICESTER* Robert Dudley, Earl of Leicester (c.1532–88), Elizabeth's
    favourite, was captain-general of the army at Tilbury when the Spanish
    invasion threatened. He died shortly after the defeat of the Armada.
117 *an abler grasp* Leicester was in fact a notably incompetent commander and had
    had to be recalled from an expedition to Holland in 1585 on grounds of
    incompetence.
123 *obliged to be plain* Bayes, too, is impatient with plainness (*The Rehearsal*
    I.i.286–7, V.i.102–6).
126 *as plenty as noun substantives* The noun substantive is the common noun found
    everywhere in any piece of writing.

Enter EARL OF LEICESTER, *the* GOVERNOR, *and others*

LEICESTER
How's this my friends! is't thus your new fledg'd zeal
And plumed valour moulds in roosted sloth?
Why dimly glimmers that heroic flame,
Whose red'ning blaze by patriot spirit fed,　　　　　130
Should be the beacon of a kindling realm?
Can the quick current of a patriot heart,
Thus stagnate in a cold and weedy converse,
Or freeze in tideless inactivity?
No! rather let the fountain of your valour　　　　　135
Spring through each stream of enterprise,
Each petty channel of conducive daring,
Till the full torrent of your foaming wrath
O'erwhelm the flats of sunk hostility!

PUFF
There it is, – followed up!　　　　　140

SIR WALTER
No more! the fresh'ning breath of thy rebuke
Hath filled the swelling canvas of our souls!
And thus, though fate should cut the cable of

All take hands

Our topmost hopes, in friendship's closing line
We'll grapple with despair, and if we fall,　　　　　145
We'll fall in Glory's wake!

LEICESTER
There spoke Old England's genius!
Then, are we all resolved?

128　*moulds* 1781 (moults L)
133　*weedy* 1781 (Pond-like L)
140　*There...up!* 1781 (*omits* L)
144　*topmost* 1781 (*omits* L)

128　*moulds* The reading 'moults' evidently suits plumes in decay and perhaps for
this reason was preferred by the copyist of L, who may nevertheless have had in
his original the *difficilior lectio* 'moulds'. This is a rare verb meaning 'grows
mouldy', which suits the *slowness* of sloth, and seems the kind of deliberately
odd and self-conscious word Puff would like. It goes with 'stagnate' at II.ii.133.
137　*conducive* contributive
139　*flats* low lying ground
142　*souls* Puff's rhetorical replacement for 'sails'
144　*closing line* The naval metaphor persists, and as they take hands (see note at
II.ii.62) we are to think of a defensive line of ships.

ALL
   We are – all resolved.

LEICESTER
   To conquer – or be free?   150

ALL
   To conquer, or be free.

LEICESTER
   All?

ALL
   All.

DANGLE
   Nem. con. egad!

PUFF
   O yes, where they *do* agree on the stage, their unanimity is 155
   wonderful.

LEICESTER
   Then, let's embrace – and now – [*kneels*]

SNEER
   What the plague, is he going to pray?

PUFF
   Yes, hush! – in great emergencies, there is nothing like a
   prayer!   160

LEICESTER
   O mighty Mars!

DANGLE
   But why should he pray to *Mars?*

PUFF
   Hush!

LEICESTER
   If in thy homage bred,
   Each point of discipline I've still observed;   165
   Nor but by due promotion, and the right
   Of service, to the rank of Major-General
   Have risen; assist thy votary now!

GOVENOR
   Yet do not rise, – hear me! [*kneels*]

MASTER OF HORSE
   And me! [*kneels*]   170

---

170 *And me!* 1781 (*omits* L)

---

154 *Nem. con. nemine contradicente*, no one objecting, a standard, workaday phrase
    hardly matching the awesomeness of the moment
170 *And me* In L the Master of Horse is not one of the kneelers, but the scene
    obviously went so well on stage that he is added in 1781 to make the thing even
    more ludicrous, as is Puff's instruction at II.ii.174.

KNIGHT
   And me! [*kneels*]
SIR WALTER
   And me! [*kneels*]
SIR CHRISTOPHER
   And me! [*kneels*]
PUFF
   Now, pray all together.
ALL
   Behold thy votaries submissive beg,   175
   That thou wilt deign to grant them all they ask;
   Assist them to accomplish all their ends,
   And sanctify whatever means they use
   To gain them!
SNEER
   A very orthodox quintetto!   180
PUFF
   Vastly well, gentlemen. – Is that well managed or not?
   Have you such a prayer as that on the stage?
SNEER
   Not exactly.
LEICESTER (*to* PUFF)
   But, Sir, you haven't settled how we are to get off here.
PUFF
   You could not go off kneeling, could you?   185
SIR WALTER (*to* PUFF)
   O no, Sir! impossible!
PUFF
   It would have a good effect ifaith, if you could! exeunt
   praying! – Yes, and would vary the established mode of
   springing off with a glance at the pit.
SNEER
   O never mind, so as you get them off, I'll answer for it the   190
   audience won't care how.

---

174 *Now . . . together.* 1781 (*omits* L)
191 *won't* L (wont 1781)

---

180 *orthodox quintetto* Originally, in L, they *were* a quintetto; but by now there are
    actually six kneelers. The prayer, asking that the end should justify the means,
    is not an orthodox request.
185 *go off kneeling* Volscius in *The Rehearsal* (III.v.103) goes off hopping, with one
    boot on and the other off. Puff's players are less pliable.
189 *with a glance at the pit* See note at Prologue 30.

PUFF

  Well then, repeat the last line standing, and go off the old
  way.

ALL

  And sanctify whatever means we use to gain them.

                                  Exeunt

DANGLE

  Bravo! a fine exit.   195

SNEER

  Well, really Mr Puff. –

PUFF

  Stay a moment. –

            The sentinels get up

1ST SENTINEL

  All this shall to Lord Burleigh's ear.

2ND SENTINEL

  'Tis meet it should.

                         Exeunt sentinels

DANGLE

  Hey! – why, I thought those fellows had been asleep?   200

PUFF

  Only a pretence, there's the art of it; they were spies of
  Lord Burleigh's.

SNEER

  – But isn't it odd, they were never taken notice of, not even
  by the commander in chief.

PUFF

  O lud, Sir, if people who want to listen, or overhear, were 205
  not always connived at in a Tragedy, there would be no
  carrying on any plot in the world.

DANGLE

  That's certain!

PUFF

  But take care, my dear Dangle, the morning gun is going to
  fire.   210

---

199 *should.* 1781 (should – The General it seems is disapprov'd L)
201–2 *they ... Burleigh's.* 1781 (I mean it to mark Lord Burleighs Character, who,
    you know was famous for his Skill in procuring Intelligence, and employ'd all
    sorts of people as Spies L)

---

198 *Lord Burleigh's ear* William Cecil, Lord Burleigh (1520–98), Elizabeth's
    Secretary of State and Lord Treasurer, whose intelligence network was famous.

Cannon fires

DANGLE
Well, that will have a fine effect.

PUFF
I think so, and helps to realize the scene. – (*cannon twice*)
What the plague! – *three* morning guns! – there never is but
one! – aye, this is always the way at the Theatre – give these
fellows a good thing, and they never know when to have   215
done with it. You have no more cannon to fire?

PROMPTER (*from within*)
No Sir.

PUFF
Now then, for soft music.

SNEER
Pray what's that for?

PUFF
It shows that TILBURINA is coming; nothing introduces you   220
a heroine like soft music. – Here she comes.

DANGLE
And her confidante, I suppose?

PUFF
To be sure: here they are – inconsolable to the minuet in
Ariadne!

Soft music
Enter TILBURINA *and* CONFIDANTE

TILBURINA
Now has the whispering breath of gentle morn,   225
Bade Nature's voice, and Nature's beauty rise;
While orient Phoebus with unborrowed hues,
Clothes the waked loveliness which all night slept

212–16 *scene . . . fire?* 1781 (Scene There are more Cannon to fire L)
214 *way* ed. (away 1781)
223–9 *here . . . fled.* 1781 (*omits* L)

---

212 *realize the scene* There was a great contemporary effort for realism in stage
    effects (see note at I.ii.197), which may have led to an undervaluing of the play
    text itself. Already in *The Rehearsal* (I.i.158–61), one of the players thinks it is
    the 'Scenes, Cloaths and Dances . . . that are essential to a Play'.
213 *What the plague* The *three* cannon do not appear in L, and were perhaps
    introduced in performance, together with Puff's anger, as an echo of the
    multiple midnight cannon in *Hamlet* (I.iv.6 sd) before the ghost appears.
223 *here they are* The first five lines of Tilburina's speech are not in L, but the
    speech clearly went well in performance and was expanded.
223–4 *minuet in Ariadne* The much admired piece which ends the overture to
    Handel's opera *Arianna in Creta* (1734).

In heavenly drapery! Darkness is fled.
Now flowers unfold their beauties to the sun,   230
And blushing, kiss the beam he sends to wake them.
The striped carnation, and the guarded rose,
The vulgar wallflower, and smart gillyflower,
The polyanthus mean – the dapper daisy,
Sweet William, and sweet marjoram, – and all   235
The tribe of single and of double pinks!
Now too, the feathered warblers tune their notes
Around, and charm the listening grove. – The lark!
The linnet! chaffinch! bullfinch! goldfinch! greenfinch!
– But O to me, no joy can they afford!   240
Nor rose, nor wallflower, nor smart gillyflower,
Nor polyanthus mean, nor dapper daisy,
Nor William sweet, nor marjoram – nor lark,
Linnet, nor all the finches of the grove!

PUFF

Your white handkerchief madam –   245

TILBURINA

I thought, Sir, I wasn't to use that till, 'heart rending woe'.

PUFF

O yes madam – at 'the finches of the grove', if you please.

TILBURINA

                              Nor lark,
Linnet, nor all the finches of the grove! (weeps)

PUFF

Vastly well madam!   250

DANGLE

Vastly well indeed!

TILBURINA

For, O too sure, heart rending woe is now
The lot of wretched Tilburina!

DANGLE

O! – 'tis too much.

SNEER

Oh! – it is indeed.   255

254 *'tis too much.* 1781 (*omits* L)
255 *it is indeed.* (it is indeed 1781; *omits* L)

230–44 *Now...grove* Tilburina's speech has distinct Miltonic echoes about it:
    Lycidas ll. 142–50 for the flowers, and more particularly the speech of Eve at
    Paradise Lost IV.641–56 for both the subject matter and the reduplicating form.
232 *guarded rose* a rose having a border or stripe of colour; also perhaps, defended
    by thorns
254 *'tis too much* See note at III.i.58.

CONFIDANTE
Be comforted sweet lady – for who knows,
But Heaven has yet some milk-white day in store.

TILBURINA
Alas, my gentle Nora,
Thy tender youth as yet hath never mourned
Love's fatal dart. – Else wouldst thou know, that when   260
The soul is sunk in comfortless despair,
It cannot taste of merriment!

DANGLE
That's certain.

CONFIDANTE
But see where your stern father comes;
It is not meet that he should find you thus.   265

PUFF
Hey, what the plague! – what a cut is here! – why, what is
become of the description of her first meeting with Don
Whiskerandos? his gallant behaviour in the sea fight, and
the simile of the canary bird?

TILBURINA
Indeed Sir, you'll find they will not be missed.   270

PUFF
Very well. – Very well!

TILBURINA
The cue ma'am if you please.

CONFIDANTE
It is not meet that he should find you thus.

TILBURINA
Thou counsel'st right, but 'tis no easy task
For barefaced grief to wear a mask of joy.   275

Enter GOVERNOR

256 *for* 1781 (*omits* L)
268 *Whiskerandos* ed. (Wiskerandos 1781; Whiskerondos L)
    behaviour 1781 (Bravery L)

---

263 *That's certain* Dangle's intervention here rather neatly completes Tilburina's
    last line.
269 *simile of the canary bird* Bayes is very fond of similes (*The Rehearsal* I.i.354,
    IV.ii.22 and II.iii.13–17): "tis the new way of writing". It is interesting to note
    that the playwright in *Ixion*, an early and fragmentarily surviving burlesque
    piece by Sheridan and his school friend Nathaniel Halhed, is called Simile.
270 *will not be missed* i.e. 'their omission will not be noticed', not 'they will not be
    omitted'

GOVERNOR
How's this – in tears? – O Tilburina, shame!
Is this a time for maudlin tenderness,
And Cupid's baby woes? – hast thou not heard
That haughty Spain's Pope-consecrated fleet
Advances to our shores, while England's fate,   280
Like a clipped guinea, trembles in the scale!

TILBURINA
Then, is the crisis of my fate at hand!
I see the fleets approach – I see –

PUFF
Now, pray gentlemen mind. – This is one of the most useful
figures we tragedy writers have, by which a hero or heroine,   285
in consideration of their being often obliged to overlook
things that *are* on the stage, is allowed to hear and see a
number of things that are not.

SNEER
Yes – a kind of poetical second sight!

PUFF
Yes – now then madam.   290

TILBURINA
                                     I see their decks
Are cleared! – I see the signal made!
The line is formed! – a cable's length asunder!
I see the frigates stationed in the rear;
And now, I hear the thunder of the guns!   295
I hear the victors' shouts – I also hear
The vanquished groan! – and now 'tis smoke – and now
I see the loose sails shiver in the wind!
I see – I see – what soon you'll see –

GOVERNOR
Hold daughter! peace! this love hath turned thy brain: 300
The Spanish fleet thou canst *not see – because*
– It is not yet in sight!

296 *victors'* (victors 1781, L)

---

277 *maudlin* mawkishly sentimental
281 *trembles in the scale* A guinea with the edge clipped would not reach its full
    weight.
287 *is allowed to hear and see* As Hamlet 'sees' his father at I.ii.184.
296 *I also hear* Notice the ludicrous change from the tone of high-pitched rhetoric to
    that of matter-of-fact report.
299 *I see – I see –* In Henry Jones' *The Earl of Essex* (1753), Raleigh also sees a great
    deal: 'I see, / I see, my lord, our utmost wish accomplish'd! / I see great Cecil
    shine . . .' (I.i).

DANGLE
Egad though, the governor seems to make no allowance for
this poetical figure you talk of.

PUFF
No, a plain matter-of-fact man – that's his character.   305

TILBURINA
But will you then refuse his offer?

GOVERNOR
I must – I will – I can – I ought – I do.

TILBURINA
Think what a noble price.

GOVERNOR
No more – you urge in vain.

TILBURINA
His liberty is all he asks.   310

SNEER
All *who* asks Mr Puff? Who is –

PUFF
Egad Sir, I can't tell. – Here has been such cutting and
slashing, I don't know where they have got to myself.

TILBURINA
Indeed Sir, you will find it will connect very well.
– And your reward secure.   315

PUFF
O, – if they hadn't been so devilish free with their cutting
here, you would have found that Don Whiskerandos has
been tampering for his liberty, and has persuaded Tilburina
to make this proposal to her father – and now pray observe
the conciseness with which the argument is conducted.   320
Egad, the *pro & con* goes as smart as hits in a fencing
match. It is indeed a sort of small-sword logic, which we
have borrowed from the French.

---

311 *Who is* – 1781 (*omits* L)
317 *Whiskerandos* ed. (Wiskerandos 1781; *omits* L)
321 *as hits* ed. (a hits 1781; as Hits L)

---

318 *tampering* secretly negotiating
321 *as smart as hits* Bayes too provides 'a Scene of sheer Wit … snip snap, hit for
     hit, as fast as can be' (*The Rehearsal* III.i.8, 12–13).
322 *small-sword*   the light rapier for rapid thrusting and parrying, as distinct from
     the heavier sabre
323 *borrowed from the French* Though a more immediate source is provided by the
     pithy exchanges between the King and Edgar in *The Battle of Hastings* (V.i):
     'Edgar: My honour and my oath – King: Thy life – Edgar: My love'.

TILBURINA
  A retreat in Spain!
GOVERNOR
  Outlawry here!   325
TILBURINA
  Your daughter's prayer!
GOVERNOR
  Your father's oath!
TILBURINA
  My lover!
GOVERNOR
  My country!
TILBURINA
  Tilburina!   330
GOVERNOR
  England!
TILBURINA
  A title!
GOVERNOR
  Honour!
TILBURINA
  A pension!
GOVERNOR
  Conscience!   335
TILBURINA
  A thousand pounds!
GOVERNOR
  Hah! thou hast touched me nearly!
PUFF
  There you see – she threw in *Tilburina*. Quick, parry quart
  with *England!* – Hah! thrust in tierce a title! – parried by
  honour. – Hah! a pension over the arm! – put by by   340
  conscience. – Then flanconade with a thousand pounds
  – and a palpable hit egad!
TILBURINA
  Canst thou –
  Reject the suppliant, *and the* daughter *too?*

338 *Tilburina.* (*Tilburina,* 1781; Tilburina L)
342 *egad!* 1781 (Egad *Sneer:* Well Push'd Indeed L)

338–41 *parry . . . pounds* The passage is full of fencing terms: 'quart' and 'tierce' are
  two of the standard positions for the sword arm; the 'flanconade' is a thrust in
  the flank.
342 *a palpable hit* Osric similarly judges one of Hamlet's thrusts at Laertes 'a hit, a
  very palpable hit' (V.ii.273).

GOVERNOR
> *No more; I would not hear thee plead in vain,*   345
> *The* father *softens – but the* governor
> *Is fixed!*   *Exit*

DANGLE
Aye, that antithesis of persons – is a most established figure.

TILBURINA
> *'Tis well, – hence then fond hopes, – fond passion hence;*
> *Duty, behold I am all over thine –*   350

WHISKERANDOS (*without*)
> *Where is my love – my –*

TILBURINA
> *Ha!*

WHISKERANDOS (*without*)
> *My beauteous enemy –*

PUFF
O dear ma'am, you must start a great deal more than that;
consider you had just determined in favour of duty – when 355
in a moment the sound of his voice revives your passion, –
overthrows your resolutions, destroys your obedience. – If
you don't express all that in your start – you do nothing at
all.

TILBURINA
Well, we'll try again!   360

DANGLE
Speaking from within has always a fine effect.

SNEER
Very.

TILBURINA
> *Behold, I am all over thine –*

WHISKERANDOS (*without*)
> *Where is my Love? – my*

TILBURINA
> *Ha! –*   365

WHISKERANDOS
> *My beauteous enemy,*

346–7 *governor Is fixed!* 1781 (Governors resolv'd L)
353 sd *without* L (*entering* 1781)
363–6 *Behold . . . enemy,* L (*omits* 1781. *These four lines are supplied from L on the
grounds that they make sense of line 360*)

356 *in a moment* Prince Volscius in Bayes' play decides as suddenly for love: 'Bless
me! how frail are all my best resolves! / How, in a moment, is my purpose
chang'd!' (*The Rehearsal* III.v.43–4).

My conquering Tilburina! (entering) How! is't thus
We meet? why are thy looks averse! what means
That falling tear – that frown of boding woe?
Hah! now indeed I am a prisoner!   370
Yes, now I feel the galling weight of these
Disgraceful chains – which, cruel Tilburina!
Thy doating captive gloried in before. –
But thou art false, and Whiskerandos is undone!

TILBURINA

O no; how little dost thou know thy Tilburina!   375

WHISKERANDOS

Art thou then true? Begone cares, doubts and fears,
I make you all a present to the winds;
And if the winds reject you – try the waves.

PUFF

The wind you know, is the established receiver of all stolen
sighs, and cast off griefs and apprehensions.   380

TILBURINA

Yet must we part – stern duty seals our doom:
Though here I call yon conscious clouds to witness,
Could I pursue the bias of my soul,
All friends, all right of parents I'd disclaim,
And thou, my Whiskerandos, should'st be father   385
And mother, brother, cousin, uncle, aunt,
And friend to me!

WHISKERANDOS

O matchless excellence! – and must we part?
Well, if – we must – we must – and in that case,
The less is said the better.   390

PUFF

Hey day! here's a cut! – What, are all the mutual
protestations out?

TILBURINA

Now, pray Sir, don't interrupt us just here, you ruin our
feelings.

367 *(entering) How!* (How! 1781; (Enter Don) Ha! L)
374 *Whiskerandos* ed. (Wiskerandos 1781; Whiskerantes L)
379–80 *stolen sighs, and* 1781 *(omits* L)
381 *part* L (part? 1781)
385 *Whiskerandos* ed. (Wiskerandos 1781; Wiskerantes L)

---

377 *present to the winds* Similarly Essex in *The Earl of Essex* II: 'I scorn the blaze of
    courts, the pomp of kings; / I give them to the winds'.
383 *bias* predisposition
385–6 *father . . . aunt* There is a similar abundance of relations at III.i.58–60.

PUFF

> *Your* feelings! – but zounds, *my* feelings, ma'am!   395

SNEER

No; pray don't interrupt them.

WHISKERANDOS

> *One last embrace –*

TILBURINA

> *Now, – farewell, for ever.*

WHISKERANDOS

> *For ever!*

TILBURINA

> *Aye for ever.*   *Going* 400

PUFF

S'death and fury! – Gadslife! Sir! Madam! if you go out without the parting look, you might as well dance out – Here, here!

CONFIDANTE

But pray Sir, how am *I* to get off here?

PUFF

You, pshaw! what the devil signifies how *you* get off! edge   405
away at the top, or where you will – (*pushes the* CONFI-
DANTE *off*) Now ma'am you see –

TILBURINA

We understand you Sir.
Aye, for ever.

BOTH

> *Ohh!*   410

> *Turning back and exeunt. Scene closes*

DANGLE

O charming!

PUFF

Hey! – 'tis pretty well I believe – you see I don't attempt to strike out anything new – but I take it I improve on the established modes.

---

395 *Your . . . ma'am!* 1781 (*omits* L)
401 *S'death . . . fury!* – 1781 (*omits* L)
405 *You,* 1781 (*omits* L)

401–2 *if you go . . . look* Bayes, too, is furious that Prince Pretty-man doesn't enter
properly: 'I vow to gad, Mr – a – I would not give a button for my Play, now you
have done this' (*The Rehearsal* III.iv.5–8).
404–6 *But . . . top* Bayes has trouble with a question about getting off, and deals with
it similarly peremptorily (*The Rehearsal* V.i.344–52). Puff's advice to the
actress here is to exit unobtrusively right at the back of the main stage.

SNEER

You do indeed. – But pray is not Queen Elizabeth to   415
appear?

PUFF

No not once – but she is to be talked of for ever; so that
egad you'll think a hundred times that she is on the point of
coming in.

SNEER

Hang it, I think it's a pity to keep *her* in the green room all   420
the night.

PUFF

O no, that always has a fine effect – it keeps up expectation.

DANGLE

But are we not to have a battle?

PUFF

Yes, yes, you will have a battle at last, but, egad, it's not to
be by land – but by sea – and that is the only quite new thing   425
in the piece.

DANGLE

What, Drake at the Armada, hey?

PUFF

Yes, ifaith – fire ships and all – then we shall end with the
procession. – Hey! that will do I think.

SNEER

No doubt on't.   430

PUFF

Come, we must not lose time – so now for the UNDERPLOT.

SNEER

What the plague, have you another plot?

PUFF

O lord, yes – ever while you live have two plots to your
tragedy. – The grand point in managing them is only to let
your underplot have as little connection with your main   435
plot as possible. – I flatter myself nothing can be more
distinct than mine, for as in my chief plot, the characters
are all great people – I have laid my underplot in low
life – and as the former is to end in deep distress, I make the
other end as happy as a farce. – [*calls out*] Now Mr   440
Hopkins, as soon as you please.

420 *it's* (its 1781, L)

---

420 *green room* See note at I.ii.323.
428 *fire ships* Against the Armada the English used old ships filled with
    inflammable material, which were then floated downwind towards the Spanish
    ships.

Enter UNDER PROMPTER

UNDER PROMPTER
Sir, the carpenter says it is impossible you can go to the
Park scene yet.

PUFF
The Park scene! No – I mean the description scene here, in
the wood.   445

UNDER PROMPTER
Sir, the performers have cut it out.

PUFF
Cut it out!

UNDER PROMPTER
Yes Sir.

PUFF
What! the whole account of Queen Elizabeth?

UNDER PROMPTER
Yes Sir.   450

PUFF
And the description of her horse and side-saddle?

UNDER PROMPTER
Yes Sir.

PUFF
So, so, this is very fine indeed! [*calls out*] Mr Hopkins, how
the plague could you suffer this?

HOPKINS (*from within*)
Sir, indeed the pruning knife –   455

PUFF
The pruning knife – zounds the axe! why, here has been
such lopping and topping. I shan't have the bare trunk of
my play left presently. – Very well, Sir – the performers
must do as they please, but upon my soul, I'll print it every
word.   460

SNEER
That I would indeed.

PUFF
Very well – Sir – then we must go on – zounds! I would not
have parted with the description of the horse! – Well, Sir, go
on – Sir, it was one of the finest and most laboured
things – Very well, Sir, let them go on – there you had him   465
and his accoutrements from the bit to the crupper – very
well, Sir, we must go to the Park scene.

453 *Mr Hopkins* See note at II.i.59.
466 *crupper* strap looped under the horse's tail

UNDER PROMPTER

Sir, there is the point; the carpenters say that unless there is
some business put in here before the drop, they shan't have
time to clear away the fort, or sink Gravesend and the river.   470

PUFF

So! this is a pretty dilemma truly! – Gentlemen – you must
excuse me, these fellows will never be ready, unless I go
and look after them myself.

SNEER

O dear Sir – these little things will happen –

PUFF

To cut out this scene! – but I'll print it – egad, I'll print it   475
every word!

Exeunt

---

470 *or ... river.* 1781 (*omits* L)

---

469 *before the drop* What is needed is some stage business taking place in front of the
lowered curtain (the drop), so that there is time to clear the stage behind and
bring on the new scene.

470 *or sink Gravesend and the river* L omits these words here but includes them in
the longer passage with which it concludes this scene. The painted backcloth of
Gravesend and the river would have to be dropped down beneath the stage
through a cut.

471–6 *truly ... word* L has in place of the last lines of the act a much longer passage
(see Appendix) which brings on to the stage, still not Mr Hopkins, but other
workers behind the scenes. It may have been difficult, however, to go on
persuading stage staff to face an audience (though a scene shifter does say a
couple of words at III.i.76), and that was the joke: their places could not have
been filled by regular actors. Alternatively, Sheridan may have wanted to omit
the passage because its comic reference to the river gods in Puff's procession
pre-empted and qualified the effect of the genuinely splendid pageant with
which *The Critic* and Puff's play end.

475–6 *I'll ... word* *The Critic* itself, it is clear, was often cut in performance, though
printed entire, because it was rather long for an afterpiece (see note at
I.i.319–20; Mrs Dangle too thinks Sir Fretful's tragedy 'a little too long':
I.i.305–6), and because some references or parts were no longer topical or no
longer pleased. George Sigmond comments in 1848 of the discovery scene at the
beginning of Act III that it is 'almost unknown to the theatrical world, as it is
rarely, if ever performed'.

Act III, Scene i

Before the curtain

Enter PUFF, SNEER, *and* DANGLE

PUFF
  Well, we are ready – now then for the justices.

    Curtain rises; justices, constables &c. discovered

SNEER
  This, I suppose, is a sort of senate scene.
PUFF
  To be sure – there has not been one yet.
DANGLE
  It is the underplot, isn't it?
PUFF
  Yes. What, gentlemen, do you mean to go at once to the   5
  discovery scene?
JUSTICE
  If you please, Sir.
PUFF
  O very well – harkee, I don't choose to say anything more,
  but ifaith, they have mangled my play in a most shocking
  manner!   10
DANGLE
  It's a great pity!
PUFF
  Now then, Mr Justice, if you please.
JUSTICE
  Are all the volunteers without?
CONSTABLE   *They are.*
  Some ten in fetters, and some twenty drunk.
JUSTICE
  Attends the youth, whose most opprobrious fame   15
  And clear convicted crimes have stamped him soldier?

---

1 *Well...justices.* 1781 (*omits* L)
3 *To...yet.* 1781 (*omits* L)

---

1 sd *justices, constables &c* V.i of *The Rehearsal* opens with a grand scene of state.
6 *discovery scene* scene in which some dramatic revelation occurs

CONSTABLE
> *He waits your pleasure; eager to repay*
> *The blest reprieve that sends him to the fields*
> *Of glory, there to raise his branded hand*
> *In honour's cause.*

JUSTICE   *'Tis well – 'tis Justice arms him!*   20
> *O! may he now defend his country's laws*
> *With half the spirit he has broke them all!*
> *If 'tis your worship's pleasure, bid him enter.*

CONSTABLE
> *I fly, the herald of your will.*

Exit CONSTABLE

PUFF [*to* CONSTABLE]
> Quick, Sir! –   25

SNEER
> But, Mr Puff, I think not only the Justice, but the clown seems to talk in as high a style as the first hero among them.

PUFF
> Heaven forbid they should not in a free country! – Sir, I am not for making slavish distinctions, and giving all the fine language to the upper sort of people.   30

DANGLE
> That's very noble in you indeed.

Enter JUSTICE'S LADY

PUFF
> Now pray mark this scene.

LADY
> *Forgive this interruption, good my love;*
> *But as I just now passed a pris'ner youth*
> *Whom rude hands hither led, strange bodings seized*   35
> *My fluttering heart, and to myself I said,*

19–22 *there … all!* 1781 (*a passage that seems to correspond to this has been heavily deleted in* L)
34 *passed* (past, 1781; past L)

---

19 *branded hand* The boy has been branded as punishment for a criminal offence. There were no doubt soldiers in the audience; certainly there had been martial fervour in the air a few months before the first performance of *The Critic*.
25 *Quick, Sir* The constable is plainly ambling off in rather a leisurely way, in spite of his words about flying.
35 *rude* rough
    bodings premonitions

An if our TOM had lived, he'd surely been
This stripling's height!

JUSTICE

Ha! sure some powerful sympathy directs
Us both –   40

Enter SON *and* CONSTABLE

[to SON*] What is thy name?*

SON

My name's TOM JENKINS – alias, *have I none –*
Though orphaned, and without a friend!

JUSTICE

Thy parents?

SON

My father dwelt in Rochester – and was,   45
As I have heard – a fishmonger – no more.

PUFF

What, Sir, do you leave out the account of your birth,
parentage and education?

SON

They have settled it so, Sir, here.

PUFF

Oh! oh!   50

LADY

How loudly nature whispers to my heart!
Had he no other name?

---

37 *TOM* 1781 (Jack L)
42 *TOM JENKINS* 1781 (John Wilkins L)
45–6 *and...more.* 1781 (*omits with a heavily deleted passage, part of which*
   contains the Lady's lines at III.i.51–2 L)
51 *How...heart!* 1781 (*omits L*)

---

37 *if our TOM had lived* The discovery scene in Act II of John Home's popular
   tragedy *Douglas* (1756) gives us the mother, Lady Randolph, saying that if her
   son had lived 'He might have been like this young gallant stranger / And paired
   with him in features and in shape'. The young stranger is in fact her son, who
   has been brought up by a shepherd called Old Norval. Lord Randolph, who is
   not his father (Douglas is), asks the boy's name and has the famous lines,
   parodied at III.i.42, as answer: 'My name is Norval: on the Grampian
   Hills / My father feeds his flocks'. Originally, in L, Tom was Jack, or more
   formally, John Wilkins.
46 *a fishmonger* Hamlet, feigning madness, mistakes Polonius for a fishmonger at
   II.ii.173; and Prince Pretty-man in Bayes' play thinks for a while that a
   fisherman was his father (*The Rehearsal* III.iv.34–9).

SON   *I've seen a bill*
Of his, signed Tomkins, *creditor.*
JUSTICE
This does indeed confirm each circumstance
The gypsy told! – Prepare!   55
SON
I do.
JUSTICE
No orphan, nor without a friend art thou –
I *am thy father,* here's *thy mother,* there
Thy uncle – this thy first cousin, and those
Are all your near relations!   60
LADY
O ecstasy of bliss!
SON
O most unlooked for happiness!
JUSTICE
O wonderful event!

            They faint alternately in each other's arms

PUFF
There, you see relationship, like murder, will out.
JUSTICE
Now let's revive – else were this joy too much!   65
But come – and we'll unfold the rest within,
And thou my boy must needs want rest and food.

53 *in L five lines of heavily deleted dialogue follow this line, between son and parents*
55 *told!* – 1781 (told – Quick loose Those ignominious bonds – L)
57 *art* L (ar't 1781)
63 *O . . . event!* – 1781 (*omits* L)
65 *Now . . . joy* 1781 (See she revives – this joy's L)
67 *my boy* 1781 (*omits* L)

52-3 *a bill . . . creditor* The name Tomkins clearly provided the 'Tom' and the
'kins' of the lost boy's present name, a reason perhaps for the change from Jack
to Tom, though it should be noted that Sheridan had a son called Tom, born in
November 1775. Tomkins did an odd thing to sign a bill of exchange as
'creditor'. Normally a bill of exchange, like a modern banknote, was signed by
the debtor, the person who promised to pay the money.

58 *I am thy father* In Cumberland's *The West Indian* (1771), Stockwell reveals
himself to be young Belcour's father in an affecting exchange (V.viii)
'*Stockwell*: I am your father. *Belcour*: My father! Do I live? *Stockwell*: I am your
father. *Belcour*: It is too much . . .'

63-5 *O wonderful . . . too much* The stage direction in L makes it clear that only the
mother faints; in 1781 the joke is improved as all three faint, with consequent
textual changes at III.i.63 and 65.

Hence may each orphan hope, as chance directs,
To find a father – where he least expects!

                                                          Exeunt

PUFF

What do you think of that?   70

DANGLE

One of the finest discovery scenes I ever saw. – Why, this
underplot would have made a tragedy itself.

SNEER

Aye, or a comedy either.

PUFF

And keeps quite clear you see of the other.

Enter scenemen, taking away the seats

PUFF

The scene remains, does it?   75

SCENEMAN

Yes, Sir.

PUFF

You are to leave one chair you know – But it is always
awkward in a tragedy to have you fellows coming in in your
playhouse liveries to remove things – I wish that could be
managed better. – So now for my mysterious yeoman.   80

Enter a BEEFEATER

BEEFEATER

Perdition catch my soul but I do love thee.

SNEER

Haven't I heard that line before?

PUFF

No, I fancy not – Where pray?

DANGLE

Yes, I think there is something like it in Othello.

PUFF

Gad! now you put me in mind on't, I believe there is – but   85
that's of no consequence – all that can be said is, that two
people happened to hit on the same thought – And
Shakespeare made use of it first, that's all.

---

80 – *So . . . yeoman.* – 1781 (*omits* L)

---

73 *or a comedy either* See note at I.i.251.
75 *the scene* the backcloth
81 *Perdition . . . thee* Othello was the mainpiece on the second night of *The Critic*,
    Monday, 1 November, and this line is quoted from III.iii.91–2.

SNEER
　Very true.

PUFF
　Now, Sir, your soliloquy – but speak more to the pit, if you　90
　please – the soliloquy always to the pit – that's a rule.

BEEFEATER
　Though hopeless love finds comfort in despair,
　It never can endure a rival's bliss!
　But soft – I am observed.　　　　　　　*Exit* BEEFEATER

DANGLE
　That's a very short soliloquy.　　　　　95

PUFF
　Yes – but it would have been a great deal longer if he had
　not been observed.

SNEER
　A most sentimental Beefeater that, Mr Puff.

PUFF
　Harkee – I would not have you be too sure that he *is* a
　Beefeater.　　　　　100

SNEER
　What! a hero in disguise?

PUFF
　No matter – I only give you a hint – But now for my
　principal character – Here he comes – LORD BURLEIGH in
　person! Pray, gentlemen, step this way – softly – I only hope
　the Lord High Treasurer is perfect – if he is but perfect!　105

　Enter LORD BURLEIGH, *goes slowly to a chair and sits*

91　*the soliloquy . . . rule.* 1781 (*omits* L)
105　*the . . . Treasurer* 1781 (he L)

95　*very short soliloquy* There is a notably brief remark by Shirly in *The Rehearsal* at II.iv.77–80, and a speech promised but prevented by the plot at V.i.151–7; Pretty-man, too, falls asleep in mid-soliloquy in Bayes' play at II.iii.8–9.

103　LORD BURLEIGH Puff's 'principal character', who says nothing, was understood as a reference to Lord North, who in the crisis of 1779 did nothing. It is surprising that what was instantly recognised (two days after the first performance, in the *Morning Post*) as a hit at the Prime Minister should have passed the censor; but, as John Loftis points out (*The London Theatre World, 1660–1800*, ed. Robert D. Hume, p. 276), the Lord Chamberlain received the manuscript of *The Critic* only the day before the first performance and not the statutory two weeks before, so that the Examiner, John Larpent, had to read it very quickly.

105　*perfect* perfectly rehearsed in his part

105　sd *Enter . . . sits* The two usurpers in *The Rehearsal* sit down significantly on 'the two great Chairs upon the Stage' (II.iv.69 sd).

SNEER

Mr Puff!

PUFF

Hush! – vastly well, Sir! vastly well! a most interesting gravity!

DANGLE

What, isn't he to speak at all?

PUFF

Egad, I thought you'd ask me that – yes it is a very likely   110
thing – that a Minister in his situation, with the whole
affairs of the nation on his head, should have time to
talk! – but hush! or you'll put him out.

SNEER

Put him out! how the plague can that be, if he's not going to
say anything?   115

PUFF

There's a reason! – why, his part is to *think*, and how the
plague do you imagine he can *think* if you keep talking?

DANGLE

That's very true upon my word!

> LORD BURLEIGH *comes forward,*
> *shakes his head and exit*

SNEER

He is very perfect indeed – Now, pray what did he mean by
that?   120

PUFF

You don't take it?

SNEER

No; I don't upon my soul.

PUFF

Why, by that shake of the head, he gave you to understand

107–8 *Sir . . . gravity!* 1781 (*omits* L)
118 *word!* 1781 (word – Now – hush – close – L)

---

109 *to speak at all* Johnson at one point suggests to Bayes that two of his characters
should 'go out again without ever speaking one word' (*The Rehearsal* V.i.191);
Pretty-man resolves something or other entirely in his sleep (II.iii.35); and two
politicians whisper because 'matters of State ought not to be divulg'd'
(II.i.69–70).
116 *There's a reason* what a foolish opinion
121 *take* understand

that even though they had more justice in their cause and
wisdom in their measures – yet, if there was not a greater   125
spirit shown on the part of the people – the country would
at last fall a sacrifice to the hostile ambition of the Spanish
monarchy.

SNEER
The devil! – did he mean all that by shaking his head?

PUFF
Every word of it – if he shook his head as I taught him.   130

DANGLE
Ah! there certainly is a vast deal to be done on the stage by
dumb show, and expression of face, and a judicious author
knows how much he may trust to it.

SNEER
O, here are some of our old acquaintance.

Enter SIR CHRISTOPHER HATTON *and* SIR WALTER RALEIGH

SIR CHRISTOPHER
My niece, and your niece too!   135
By heaven! there's witchcraft in't – He could not else
Have gained their hearts – But see where they approach;
Some horrid purpose lowering on their brows!

SIR WALTER
Let us withdraw and mark them.

                                          They withdraw

SNEER
What is all this?   140

PUFF
Ah! here has been more pruning! – but the fact is, these two
young ladies are also in love with Don Whiskerandos.
– Now, gentlemen, this scene goes entirely for what we call
SITUATION and STAGE EFFECT, by which the greatest
applause may be obtained, without the assistance of   145
language, sentiment or character: pray mark!

124-5 *even . . . measures* 1781 (tho' every thing was to be hoped for from the Justice
  of their cause, and the wisdom of their measures L)
132-3 *and a . . . it.* 1781 (*omits* L)
139 *Let . . . them.* 1781 (*omits* L)
142 *Whiskerandos* 1781 (Wiskerandos L)

---

136 *witchcraft* Othello, too, was accused of gaining Desdemona's love by witchcraft
  (I.iii.169).
145-6 *without the assistance of language* Bayes at one point does not value words
  (*The Rehearsal* V.i.3). See the text at III.i.131-3 and the note at II.ii.212.

Enter the two nieces

1ST NIECE
  Ellena here!
  She is his scorn as much as I – that is
  Some comfort still.
PUFF
  O dear madam, you are not to say that to her face! – *aside,*   150
  ma'am, *aside.* – The whole scene is to be *aside.*
1ST NIECE (*aside*)
  She is his scorn as much as I – that is
  Some comfort still!
2ND NIECE (*aside*)
  I know he prizes not Pollina's love,
  But Tilburina lords it o'er his heart.   155
1ST NIECE (*aside*)
  But see the proud destroyer of my peace.
  Revenge is all the good I've left.
2ND NIECE (*aside*)
  He comes, the false disturber of my quiet.
  Now vengeance do thy worst –

Enter DON WHISKERANDOS

WHISKERANDOS
  O hateful liberty – if thus in vain   160
  I seek my Tilburina!
BOTH NIECES   *And ever shalt!*

SIR CHRISTOPHER HATTON
and SIR WALTER RALEIGH *come forward*

SIR CHRISTOPHER AND SIR WALTER
  Hold! we will avenge you.
WHISKERANDOS
  Hold you – *or see your nieces bleed!*

151–2 *be aside . . . I* – 1781 (aside. *1st Niece:* Very true Sir. *Puff:* She is his scorn as
    much as I . . . L)
154 *I . . . love,* 1781 (He scorns, he knows Pollena's Love L)
160 *O . . . thus* 1781 (*omits* L)
163 *bleed!* ed. (bleed.! 1781; bleed. – L)

The two nieces draw their two daggers to strike DON
WHISKERANDOS, *the two uncles at the instant with their two
swords drawn, catch their two nieces' arms, and turn the points
of their swords to* DON WHISKERANDOS, *who immediately draws
two daggers, and holds them to the two nieces' bosoms*

PUFF
There's situation for you! – there's an heroic group! – You
see the ladies can't stab Whiskerandos – he durst not strike   165
them for fear of their uncles – the uncles durst not kill him,
because of their nieces – I have them all at a deadlock! – for
every one of them is afraid to let go first.
SNEER
Why, then they must stand there for ever.
PUFF
So they would, if I hadn't a very fine contrivance for't –   170
Now mind –

Enter BEEFEATER *with his halberd*

BEEFEATER
*In the Queen's name I charge you all to drop
Your swords and daggers!*

They drop their swords and daggers

SNEER
That is a contrivance indeed.
PUFF
Aye – in the Queen's name.   175
SIR CHRISTOPHER
Come niece!
SIR WALTER
Come niece!

Exeunt with the two nieces

WHISKERANDOS
What's he who bids us thus renounce our guard?
BEEFEATER
Thou must do more, renounce thy love!

164 *group* 1781 (grief L)
167 *I... deadlock!* 1781 (*these words appear at III.i.165 between* see *and the in* L)
174–5 *That... name.* 1781 (*omits* L)

---

163 sd The tableau effect here reminds one of Bayes' 'battel in *Recitativo*' (*The
Rehearsal* V.i.198). Bayes, too, in his turn has the *audience* at a deadlock (*The
Rehearsal* I.i.352).

WHISKERANDOS
Thou liest – base Beefeater!
BEEFEATER   *Ha! Hell! the lie!*   180
By heaven thou'st rous'd the lion in my heart!
Off yeoman's habit – base disguise! – off! off!

> *Discovers himself by throwing off his upper dress,*
> *and appearing in a very fine waistcoat*

Am I a Beefeater now?
Or beams my crest as terrible as when
In Biscay's Bay I took thy captive sloop?   185
PUFF
There, egad! he comes out to be the very Captain of the
privateer who had taken Whiskerandos prisoner – and was
himself an old lover of Tilburina's.
DANGLE
Admirably managed indeed.
PUFF
Now, stand out of their way.   190
WHISKERANDOS
I thank thee fortune! that hast thus bestowed
A weapon to chastise this insolent.

> *Takes up one of the swords*

BEEFEATER
I take thy challenge, Spaniard, and I thank
Thee Fortune too! –

> *Takes up the other sword*

DANGLE
That's excellently contrived! – it seems as if the two uncles   195
had left their swords on purpose for them.
PUFF
No, egad, they could not help leaving them.
WHISKERANDOS
Vengeance and Tilburina!
BEEFEATER   *Exactly so –*

180 *Hell!* 1781 (*omits* L)
182 *– off! off!* 1781 (*omits* L)
185 *sloop?* (sloop. 1781, L)
193–7 *Spaniard ... them.* 1781 (*omits* L)
198 *Exactly so –* 1781 (*omits* L)

192 *insolent* insolent man

They fight – and after the usual number of wounds given,
                     DON WHISKERANDOS *falls*

WHISKERANDOS
  O cursed parry! – that last thrust in tierce
  Was fatal – Captain, thou hast fenced well!   200
  And Whiskerandos quits this bustling scene
  For all eter –
BEEFEATER
  – nity – He would have added, but stern death
  Cut short his being, and the noun at once!
PUFF
  O, my dear Sir, you are too slow, now mind me. – Sir, shall I   205
  trouble you to die again?
WHISKERANDOS
  And Whiskerandos quits this bustling scene
  For all eter –
BEEFEATER
  – nity – He would have added –
PUFF
  No, Sir – that's not it – once more if you please –   210
WHISKERANDOS
  I wish, Sir – you would practise this without me – I can't
  stay dying here all night.
PUFF
  Very well, we'll go over it by and by – I must humour these
  gentlemen!
                          Exit DON WHISKERANDOS
BEEFEATER
  Farewell – brave Spaniard! and when next –   215

203 *stern* 1781 (*omits* L)
204 *noun* 1781 (Noise L)
213 *humour* 1781 (recover L)
215–16 *and ... Sir,* 1781 (*omits* L)

---

202 *For all eter –* Hamlet dies his story untold at the end of Shakespeare's play; but a
    closer parallel is with Henry Brooke's *Gustavus Vasa* (1739), in which a dying
    man is literally stopped short in the middle of a word (III.ii).
205 *you are too slow* The Beefeater did not take up his cue smartly enough, so
    leaving an embarrassing pause between the first two and last two syllables of
    'eternity'. One is bound to say that the cue instantly taken would only produce
    another kind of absurdity. Little wonder even Puff has difficulty.
212 *stay ... night* Whiskerandos' refusal to 'stay dying here all night' originated with
    a wearied remark at rehearsal by the actor John Bannister, according to George
    Sigmond in his *Memoir* of Sheridan's life prefacing the 1848 *Works*. The words
    appear in L as well as 1781, but the Larpent MS was still of course, being
    written in the latest stages of rehearsal (see pp. xiv and xxv).

PUFF

Dear Sir, you needn't speak that speech as the body has walked off.

BEEFEATER

That's true, Sir – then I'll join the fleet.

PUFF

If you please   *Exit* BEEFEATER

Now, who comes on?   220

Enter GOVERNOR, *with his hair properly disordered*

GOVERNOR

A hemisphere of evil planets reign!
And every planet sheds contagious frenzy!
My Spanish prisoner is slain! my daughter,
Meeting the dead corse borne along – has gone
Distract!

A loud flourish of trumpets

But hark, I am summoned to the fort,   225
Perhaps the fleets have met! amazing crisis!
O Tilburina! from thy aged father's beard
Thou'st plucked the few brown hairs which time had left!

Exit GOVERNOR

SNEER

Poor gentleman!

PUFF

Yes – and no one to blame but his daughter!   230

DANGLE

And the planets –

PUFF

True. – Now enter Tilburina! –

SNEER

Egad, the business comes on quick here.

221-2 *reign ... frenzy!* 1781 (Sure are reigning, Shedding their baneful influence round – L)

226 *amazing crisis!* 1781 (*omits* L)

227-8 *aged ... left!* 1781 (Fathers Beard which time had left, Thou's't pluck'd the few Black Hairs L)

229-32 *Poor ... True.* – 1781 (*omits* L)

216-17 *body has walked off* The dead also walk off in *The Rehearsal* (V.i.346-52); at one point they even dance (II.v.7-10).

230 *to blame but his daughter* The Governor, who has just entered with his hair disordered, begins to remind us of King Lear.

PUFF

Yes, Sir – now she comes in stark mad in white satin.

SNEER

Why in white satin?   235

PUFF

O Lord, Sir – when a heroine goes mad, she always goes into
white satin – don't she, Dangle?

DANGLE

Always – it's a rule.

PUFF

Yes – here it is – (*looking at the book*) 'Enter Tilburina stark
mad in white satin, and her confidante stark mad in white   240
linen.'

Enter TILBURINA *and* CONFIDANTE *mad,*
according to custom

SNEER

But what the deuce, is the confidante to be mad too?

PUFF

To be sure she is, the confidante is always to do whatever
her mistress does; weep when she weeps, smile when she
smiles, go mad when she goes mad. – Now madam confi-   245
dante – but – keep your madness in the background, if you
please.

TILBURINA

The wind whistles – the moon rises – see
They have killed my squirrel in his cage!
Is this a grasshopper! – Ha! no, it is my   250
Whiskerandos – you shall not keep him –
I know you have him in your pocket –
An oyster may be crossed in love! – Who says
A whale's a bird? – Ha! did you call, my love?

238–41 *it's . . . linen.'* 1781 (*omits* L)
251 *Whiskerandos* 1781 (Ferolo L)

239–41 *Enter . . . linen* This was a famously comic episode in *The Critic*, and is
emphasised in 1781 by an addition to the L text.
248–56 *The wind . . . nowhere* Tilburina's mad speech echoes Ophelia's madness
(*Hamlet* IV.v), perhaps played in white satin on the first night of *The Critic*.
The dead squirrel would also probably remind the audience of the widow
entering with a dead squirrel in V.iii of Richard Steele's *The Funeral* (1701),
one of the earliest comedies to turn away from the licentious wit of the
Restoration stage.

– He's here! He's there! – He's everywhere!   255
Ah me! He's nowhere!

Exit TILBURINA [*and* CONFIDANTE]

PUFF
There, do you ever desire to see anybody madder than that?

SNEER
Never while I live!

PUFF
You observed how she mangled the metre?

DANGLE
Yes – egad, it was the first thing made me suspect she was   260
out of her senses.

SNEER
And pray what becomes of her?

PUFF
She is gone to throw herself into the sea to be sure – and
that brings us at once to the scene of action, and so to my
catastrophe – my sea-fight, I mean.   265

SNEER
What, you bring that in at last?

PUFF
Yes – yes – you know my play is *called* the *Spanish Armada*,
otherwise, egad, I have no occasion for the battle at all.
– Now then for my magnificence! – my battle! – my noise! –
and my procession! – [*calls out*] You are all ready?   270

PROMPTER (*within*)
Yes, Sir.

PUFF
Is the Thames dressed?

259–69 *You . . . noise!* – 1781 (Now then for my magnificence – My Battle L)

---

263 *throw . . . sea* It is falsely reported in Bayes' play that Lardella was 'drown'd at
Sea, and had a wave for her Winding sheet' (*The Rehearsal* IV.i.92); Cloris,
however, really does drown herself (V.i.375). The death of Ophelia in *Hamlet* is
echoed too.

265 *catastrophe* dénouement

267 *called the Spanish Armada* 'Why Mr Cumberland has chosen to call this play
The battle of Hastings, we do not see. To be sure we hear something of such a
battle in the last act, but almost the whole of the tragedy consists of love-scenes
between a disguised prince, and a couple of fond maidens' (*Scot's Magazine*,
February 1778).

269 *my magnificence* Puff is as proud of his show as Bayes of his (*The Rehearsal*
V.i.1–7).

271 *Yes, Sir* See note at II.i.59.

272 *Thames dressed* One is reminded of Bayes' similarly casual and bizarre question
'is the Lance fill'd with Wine?' (*The Rehearsal* III.v.162).

Enter THAMES *with two attendants*

THAMES
Here I am, Sir.
PUFF
Very well indeed – See, gentlemen, there's a river for you!
– This is blending a little of the masque with my tragedy –   275
a new fancy you know – and very useful in my case; for as
there *must be* a *procession*, I suppose Thames and all his
tributary rivers to compliment Britannia with a fete in
honour of the victory.
SNEER
But pray, who are these gentlemen in green with him?   280
PUFF
Those? – those are his banks.
SNEER
His banks?
PUFF
Yes, one crowned with alders and the other with a villa! –
you take the allusions? – but hey! what the plague! you have
got both your banks on one side – Here Sir, come   285
round – Ever while you live, Thames, go between your

275–9 – *This . . . victory.* – 1781 (*omits* L)
280 *him?* (him. 1781; him L)
283–4 *one . . . allusions?* 1781 (*omits* L)
285–6 *Here . . . round* 1781 (*omits* L)

---

283 *one . . . villa* It was fashionable to have a house out of town, on the north bank of
the river west of London; and on the Surrey side, south of the river, were some
of the alder coppices grown for the use of the gunpowder mills at Chilworth,
near Guildford (*Victoria County History of Surrey*, vol. 2, p. 576). Evelyn, a
hundred years before *The Critic*, remarks on the excellence of alder for the
manufacture of gunpowder (*Sylva*, 1664, p. 39); and William Gilpin in 1791
describes the country south of the Thames at this point: 'He who would see the
Alder in perfection must follow the banks of the Mole in Surrey, through the
sweet vales of Dorking and Mickleham into the groves of Esher' (C. E. Salmon,
Flora of Surrey, 1931, p. 585). Pope took the lease of his villa at Twickenham a
little north of Esher in 1717. Garrick too had a house right on the bank of the
river at Hampton, and Walpole, thirty years after Pope, acquired what was to
become his 'little Gothic castle' at Strawberry Hill. Walpole was famous for
Strawberry Hill and for his letters: one of his principal correspondents was the
Countess of Upper Ossory (wife of the 2nd Earl), whose brother-in-law wrote
the Prologue to *The Critic*, which Walpole in a letter to Lady Ossory of 6
December 1779 described as 'a short, just, and compendious history of the
English stage'.

banks. *(bell rings)* – There, so! now for't! – Stand aside my
dear friends! – away Thames!

> *Exit* THAMES *between his banks*

*Flourish of drums – trumpets – cannon, &c.&c. Scene changes
to the sea – the fleets engage – the music plays 'Britons strike
home'. – Spanish fleet destroyed by fire-ships, &c. – English
fleet advances – music plays 'Rule Britannia'. – The procession
of all the English rivers and their tributaries with their
emblems, &c. begins with Handel's Water Music – ends with a
chorus, to the march in Judas Maccabaeus. – During this scene,*
PUFF *directs and applauds everything – then*

PUFF

Well, pretty well – but not quite perfect – so ladies and
gentlemen, if you please, we'll rehearse this piece again   290
tomorrow.

> *Curtain drops*

287-91 – *There . . . tomorrow.* 1781(Now for't. L)

286-7 *go between your banks* Bayes has a dance where Earth, Sun and Moon change
    places (*The Rehearsal* V.i.289–95).
287 *bell rings* The bell rang at the beginning of Puff's play to warn the audience that
    the play itself was about to begin (II.i.64 sd); it rings here to signal that Puff's
    play is ended and to release the audience, no doubt, into enthusiastic
    participation in the patriotic musical pageantry with which the evening's
    entertainment closes (see pp. xi and xvii).
288 sd The song 'Britons strike home', set by Purcell, is from an adaptation of
    Fletcher's *Bonduca* (1614), first played in 1696 and revived by George Colman
    the Elder at the Theatre Royal, Haymarket in 1778. James Thomson's words for
    'Rule, Britannia' were set to music by Thomas Arne for the masque *Alfred* (cf.
    III.i.275), composed by Thomson and David Mallet in 1740. Handel's *Water
    Music* was composed in about 1717 and his oratorio *Judas Maccabaeus* in 1747.
    Puff to the last interferes with his help, like Bayes (see note at I.ii.38 sd) though
    he seems also to modulate here into a non-burlesque conductor of the closing
    patriotic scene. See note at I.ii.197 and p. xvi.
284-91 *Well . . . tomorrow* Puff's closing words to the 'ladies and gentlemen' are
    perhaps as much to the audience as to the actors in his play, and he speaks
    finally (very much unlike Bayes) with almost the authority of the manager of
    the theatre himself.

Appendix

In place of Act II, scene ii, lines 471–6 in the 1781 text,
the Larpent MS has a much longer passage

truly ... word! 1781 (indeed – do call the head Carpenter to me
Under Prompter: Mr Butler (*enter Carpenter dressed*) Here he is
Sir   *Puff:* Hey – this the head Carpenter   *Under Prompter:* Yes Sir
He was to have walk'd as one of the Generals at the review,
for the truth is Sir your Tragedy employs every body in the
Company   *Puff:* Then Pray Mr General, or Mr Carpenter what is
all this?   *Carpenter:* Why Sir you only Consider what my Men
have to do – they have got to remove Tilbury Fort with the Cannon,
and to sink Gravesend and the River, and I only desire three
minutes to do it in   *Puff:* Ah, and they have cut out the
Scene   *Carpenter:* Besides, could I manage it in less, I question if
the Lamplighters could clear Away the Sun in time   *Puff:* Do, call
one of them here   *Under Prompter:* Master Lamplighter (*from
without*) Mr Goodwin   *Langley:* Here (*enter Lamplighter as a
River God with a Page holding up his train*)   *Puff:* Sir, your most
obedient Servant – who the Devils this?   *Under Prompter:* The
Master Lamplighter Sir – he does one of the River Gods in the
Procession   *Puff:* O, a River God is he – Well Sir, you want time
here I understand   *Lamplighter:* Three Minutes at least Sir, unless
you have a Mind to burn the Fort   *Puff:* Then they have cut out
the Scene   *Carpenter:* Lord Sir there only wants a little Business
to be put in here just as long as while we have been speaking
will do it   *Puff:* What then are you all ready now?   *Prompter:*
(*behind*) Yes, all Clear   *Puff:* O, then we'll easily manage
it   *Under Prompter:* Clear the Stage   *Puff:* And do General keep
a Sharp look out, and beg the River God, not to spare his Oil in
the last Scene, it must be brilliant – Gentlemen I beg a thousand
Pardons but –   *Sneer:* O dear these little things will happen)